LATIMER STUDIES 20 – 21

THE THIRTY-NINE ARTICLES: THEIR PLACE AND USE TODAY

BY J. I. PACKER

With the Text of the Articles, Textual Notes, and an Appendix on Supplementing the Articles

BY R. T. BECKWITH

The Latimer Trust

First published: Oxford, Latimer House 1984 ISBN   0-946307-19-9/20-2

The Thirty-Nine Articles: Their Place and Use Today © James I. Packer and Roger T. Beckwith.

Second edition: London 2006

ISBN 0-946307-56-3

EAN   9780946307562

Published by the Latimer Trust

c/o Oak Hill College

London N14 4PS

www.latimertrust.org

CONTENTS

PREFACE to the FIRST EDITION

As I hinted in an earlier Latimer Study (*A Kind of Noah's Ark? The Anglican Commitment to Comprehensiveness*, 1981), I am an Anglican not so much by sentiment or affection as by conviction. John Henry Newman did not particularly like the Church of Rome as he saw it from outside, and later as he experienced it, but he joined it out of conviction and never thereafter wavered in his certainty that he was in the right place.   I cannot say that I ever particularly liked the Church of England as I found it, but I remain an Anglican out of conviction that here is the right place, for here I possess the truest, wisest and potentially richest heritage in all Christendom.   One factor which holds me steady at this point is my veneration (the word is not too strong) for the Thirty-nine Articles, which seem to me not only to catch the substance and spirit of biblical Christianity superbly well, but also to provide as apt a model of the way to confess the faith in a divided Christendom as the world has yet seen.   In this essay I try to show how the Articles should be viewed and received, and how they can be used to enrich the faith of Anglicans in general and of Anglican evangelicals in particular.

Though I am now a Canadian citizen, I retain my British passport; and therefore I hope it will not seem strange that, though I now serve in the Anglican Church of Canada, I should write as a minister of the Church of England.

Sections of the essay appeared in an earlier form in *The Thirty-Nine Articles* (London: Falcon, 1961), *The Articles of the Church of England* (London: Mowbrays, 1964; copyright, used by permission), and *A Guide to The Articles Today* (London: Church Book Room Press, 1969); all of which are now out of print.

J. I. PACKER

Since the 1662 Book of Common Prayer is less in people's hands than it was (with the advent of the *Alternative Service Book,* due to remain in use until 1990), it has been thought wise to reprint the text of the 39 Articles at the beginning of this study, and a few notes have been added, where necessary, for the explanation of technical or old-fashioned words.   At the end of the study an appendix on Supplementing the Articles has been added, addressing itself to further issues which have come into prominence since the Articles were composed.

R. T. BECKWITH

PREFACE to the SECOND EDITION

Much has changed within the Church of England since Jim Packer and Roger Beckwith first wrote this booklet, more than twenty years ago.   For example, the *Alternative Service Book* has been consigned to the liturgical scrap heap; the ordination of women is now an established fact; the Lambeth Conferences of 1958 and 1968 are long-since forgotten; and the innovative 1975 Declaration of Assent has grown into an authoritative and defining text for the Church of England's identity.

Yet this study remains much in demand and as timely as ever.   As the doctrinal drift of the Church of England continues apace, so does our ignorance of the Thirty-nine Articles.   Most of the younger clergy (in fact, many of those still under retirement age) have never studied them nor been taught to value them. Packer and Beckwith demonstrate clearly why the Articles must once again be given a voice within the Church, not merely as an historical curiosity but an authoritative doctrinal statement.   As the wider Anglican Communion works towards an 'Anglican Covenant' in the aftermath of the 2004 *Windsor Report,* it is to be hoped that the Thirty-nine Articles will be given a prominent place in that agreement.   Their resurgence within Anglican life can only be of benefit to the church today.

The Publishers, 2006

THE TEXT OF THE ARTICLES

ARTICLES

Agreed upon by the Archbishops
and Bishops of both provinces
and the whole clergy in the
Convocation holden at London
in the year 1562 for the avoiding
of diversities of opinions and
for the establishing of consent
touching true religion

reprinted
by command of His Majesty
King Charles I
with his Royal Declaration
prefixed thereunto

HIS MAJESTY'S DECLARATION

BEING by God's ordinance, according to our just title, Defender of the Faith, and Supreme Governor of the Church, within these our dominions, we hold it most agreeable to this our kingly office, and our own religious zeal, to conserve and maintain the Church committed to our charge, in unity of true religion, and in the bond of peace; and not to suffer unnecessary disputations, altercations, or questions to be raised, which may nourish faction both in the Church and Commonwealth. We have therefore, upon mature deliberation, and with the advice of so many of our Bishops as might conveniently be called together, thought fit to make this Declaration following :

That the Articles of the Church of England (which have been allowed and authorized heretofore, and which our clergy generally have subscribed unto) do contain the true doctrine of the Church of England agreeable to God's Word : which we do therefore ratify and confirm, requiring all our loving subjects to continue in the uniform profession thereof, and prohibiting the least difference from the said Articles; which to that end we command to be new printed, and this our Declaration to be published therewith.

That we are Supreme Governor of the Church of England: and that if any difference arise about the external policy, concerning the injunctions, canons, and other constitutions whatsoever thereto belonging, the clergy in their Convocation is to order and settle them, having first obtained leave under our broad seal so to do: and we approving their said ordinances and constitutions; providing that none be made contrary to the laws and customs of the land.

That out of our princely care that the churchmen may do the work which is proper unto them, the bishops and clergy, from time to time in Convocation, upon their humble desire, shall have licence under our broad seal to deliberate of, and to do all such things, as, being made plain by them, and assented unto by us, shall concern the settled continuance of the doctrine and discipline of the Church of England now established; from which we will not endure any varying or departing in the least degree.

That for the present, though some differences have been ill raised, yet we take comfort in this, that all clergymen within our realm have always most willingly subscribed to the Articles established; which is an argument to us, that they all agree in the true, usual, literal meaning of the said Articles; and that even in those curious points, in which the present differences lie, men of all sorts take the Articles of the Church of England to be for them; which is an argument again, that none of them intend any desertion of the Articles established.

That therefore in these both curious and unhappy differences, which have for so many hundred years, in different times and places, exercised the Church of Christ, we will, that all further curious search be laid aside, and these disputes shut up in God's promises, as they be generally set forth to us in the holy Scriptures, and the general meaning of the Articles of the Church of England according to them. And that no man hereafter shall either print, or preach, to draw the Article aside any way, but shall submit to it in the plain and full meaning thereof : and shall not put his own sense or comment to be the meaning of the Article, but shall take it in the literal and grammatical sense.

That if any publick reader in either of our universities, or any head or master of a college, or any other person respectively in either of them, shall affix any new sense to any Article, or shall publickly read, determine, or hold any publick disputation, or suffer any such to be held either way, in either the universities or colleges respectively; or if any divine in the universities shall preach or print any thing either way, other than is already established in Convocation with our royal assent; he, or they the offenders, shall be liable to our displeasure, and the Church's censure in our commission ecclesiastical, as well as any other : and we will see there shall be due execution upon them.

ARTICLES OF RELIGION

A TABLE OF THE ARTICLES

1. Of Faith in the Holy Trinity.
2. Of Christ the Son of God.
3. Of his going down into hell.
4. Of his Resurrection.
5. Of the Holy Ghost.
6. Of the sufficiency of the Scriptures.
7. Of the Old Testament.
8. Of the three Creeds.
9. Of original or birth-sin.
10. Of free-will.
11. Of justification.
12. Of good works.
13. Of works before justification.
14. Of works of supererogation.
15. Of Christ alone without sin.
16. Of sin after baptism.
17. Of predestination and election.
18. Of obtaining salvation by Christ.
19. Of the Church.
20. Of the authority of the Church.
21. Of the authority of general councils.
22. Of purgatory.
23. Of ministering in the congregation.
24. Of speaking in the congregation.
25. Of the sacraments.
26. Of the unworthiness of ministers.
27. Of baptism.
28. Of the Lord's Supper.
29. Of the wicked which eat not the body of Christ.
30. Of both kinds.
31. Of Christ's one oblation.
32. Of the marriage of priests.
33. Of excommunicate persons.
34. Of the traditions of the Church.
35. Of the homilies.
36. Of consecrating of ministers.
37. Of civil magistrates.
38. Of Christian men's goods.
39. Of a Christian man's oath.

1. ## Of Faith in the Holy Trinity

   There is but one living and true God, everlasting, without body, parts, or passions;[1] of infinite power, wisdom, and goodness; the Maker, and Preserver of all things both visible and invisible. And in unity of this Godhead there be three Persons, of one substance, power, and eternity; the Father, the Son, and the Holy Ghost.

2. ## Of the Word or Son of God, which was made very Man [2]

   The Son, which is the Word of the Father, begotten from everlasting of the Father, the very and eternal God, and of one substance with the Father, took Man's nature in the womb of the blessed Virgin, of her substance: so that two whole and perfect natures, that is to say, the Godhead and Manhood, were joined together in one Person, never to be divided, whereof is one Christ, very God, and very Man; who truly suffered, was crucified, dead, and buried, to reconcile his Father to us, and to be a sacrifice, not only for original guilt, but also for all actual sins of men.

3. ## Of the going down of Christ into hell [3]

   As Christ died for us, and was buried, so also is it to be believed, that he went down into hell.

4. ## Of the Resurrection of Christ

   Christ did truly rise again from death, and took again his body,

---

[1] 'without ... passions', in the Latin text of the Articles *impassibilis*, means that nothing can be inflicted upon God against his will.

[2] 'very Man', 'very God' in this Article means 'true Man', 'true God'. Compare 'very God of very God', ie. 'true God from true God', in the Prayer Book translation of the Nicene Creed.

[3] 'hell', in Latin *inferi* (those below), means the place and state of the dead, without any implication that they are in torment. Compare the same expression in the Prayer Book translation of the Apostles' and Athanasian Creeds.

with flesh, bones, and all things appertaining to the perfection of Man's nature; wherewith he ascended into heaven, and there sitteth, until he return to judge all men at the last day.

5. *Of the Holy Ghost*

The Holy Ghost, proceeding from the Father and the Son, is of one substance, majesty, and glory, with the Father and the Son, very and eternal God.

6. *Of the sufficiency of the holy Scriptures for salvation*

Holy Scripture containeth all things necessary to salvation : so that whatsoever is not read therein, nor may be proved thereby, is not to be required of any man, that it should be believed as an article of the Faith, or be thought requisite or necessary to salvation. In the name of the holy Scripture we do understand those canonical books of the Old and New Testament, of whose authority was never any doubt in the Church.

Of the Names and Number of the Canonical Books

Genesis	The First Book of Chronicles
Exodus	The Second Book of Chronicles
Leviticus	The First Book of Esdras
Numbers	The Second Book of Esdras
Deuteronomy	The Book of Esther
Joshua	The Book of Job
Judges	The Psalms
Ruth	The Proverbs
The First Book of Samuel	Ecclesiastes or Preacher
The Second Book of Samuel	Cantica, or Songs of Solomon
The First Book of Kings	Four Prophets the greater
The Second Book of Kings	Twelve Prophets the less

And the other Books (as Hierome saith) the Church doth read for example of life and instruction of manners;[4] but yet doth it not apply them to establish any doctrine; such are these following:

---

[4] 'manners' is old English for 'behaviour'. 'Hierome', from whom the quotation comes, is the old spelling of the name of the great church father and biblical scholar Jerome.

The Third Book of Esdras	Baruch the Prophet
The Fourth Book of Esdras[5]	The Song of the Three Children
The Book of Tobias	The Story of Susanna
The Book of Judith	Of Bel and the Dragon
The rest of the Book of Esther	The Prayer of Manasses
The Book of Wisdom	The First Book of Maccabees
Jesus the Son of Sirach	The Second Book of Maccabees

All the Books of the New Testament, as they are commonly received, we do receive, and account them Canonical.

7.   Of the Old Testament

The Old Testament is not contrary to the New: for both in the Old and New Testament everlasting life is offered to mankind by Christ, who is the only mediator between God and man, being both God and man.   Wherefore they are not to be heard, which feign that the old Fathers did look only for transitory promises. Although the Law given from God by Moses, as touching ceremonies and rites, do not bind Christian men, nor the civil precepts thereof ought of necessity to be received in any commonwealth; yet notwithstanding, no Christian man whatsoever is free from the obedience of the commandments which are called moral.

8.   Of the three Creeds

The three Creeds, *Nicene* Creed, *Athanasius's* Creed, and that which is commonly called the *Apostles'* Creed, ought thoroughly to be received and believed: for they may be proved by most certain warrants of holy Scripture.

9.   Of original or birth-sin

Original sin standeth not in the following of Adam (as the Pelagians do vainly talk;) but it is the fault and corruption of the

---

[5] In the English Apocrypha these are called the First and Second Books of Esdras. When they are numbered as the third and fourth, Ezra and Nehemiah are being counted as the first and second.

nature of every man, that naturally is ingendered of the offspring of Adam; whereby man is very far gone from original righteousness, and is of his own nature inclined to evil, so that the flesh lusteth always contrary to the spirit; and therefore in every person born into this world, it deserveth God's wrath and damnation.   And this infection of nature doth remain, yea in them that are regenerated; whereby the lust of the flesh, called in the Greek, φρονημα σαρκοσ, which some do expound the wisdom, some sensuality, some the affection, some the desire, of the flesh, is not subject to the Law of God.   And although there is no condemnation for them that believe and are baptized, yet the apostle doth confess, that concupiscence and lust hath of itself the nature of sin.[6]

10. *Of free-will*

The condition of man after the fall of Adam is such, that he cannot turn and prepare himself, by his own natural strength and good works, to faith, and calling upon God: wherefore we have no power to do good works pleasant and acceptable to God, without the grace of God by Christ preventing us,[7] that we may have a good will, and working with us, when we have that good will.

11. *Of the justification of man*

We are accounted righteous before God, only for the merit of our Lord and Saviour Jesus Christ by faith, and not for our own works or deservings: wherefore, that we are justified by faith only is a most wholesome doctrine, and very full of comfort, as more largely is expressed in the homily of justification.[8]

12. *Of good works*

Albeit that good works, which are the fruits of faith, and follow

---

[6] The reference is to Romans 8: 5-7. Also Galatians 5: 17.
[7] 'preventing' is old English for 'preceding', 'going before', as in the collect 'Prevent us, O Lord, in all our doings with thy most gracious favour...' (Holy Communion).
[8] The 'Homily of Justification' is the one in the *First Book of Homilies* there called 'Of the Salvation of all Mankind'. It is believed to be Cranmer's work.

after justification, cannot put away our sins, and endure the severity of God's judgement; yet are they pleasing and acceptable to God in Christ, and do spring out necessarily of a true and lively faith; insomuch that by them a lively faith may be as evidently known as a tree discerned by the fruit.

13. *Of works before justification*

Works done before the grace of Christ, and the inspiration of his Spirit, are not pleasant to God, forasmuch as they spring not of faith in Jesus Christ, neither do they make men meet to receive grace, or (as the school-authors say) deserve grace of congruity:[9] yea rather, for that they are not done as God hath willed and commanded them to be done, we doubt not but they have the nature of sin.

14. *Of works of supererogation*

Voluntary works besides, over, and above, God's commandments, which they call works of supererogation, cannot be taught without arrogance and impiety: for by them men do declare, that they do not only render unto God as much as they are bound to do, but that they do more for his sake, than of bounden duty is required: whereas Christ saith plainly, When ye have done all that are commanded to you, say, We are unprofitable servants.[10]

15. *Of Christ alone without sin*

Christ in the truth of our nature was made like unto us in all things, sin only except, from which he was clearly void, both in his flesh, and in his spirit. He came to be the lamb without spot, who, by sacrifice of himself once made, should take away the sins of the world, and sin, as Saint John saith, was not in him. But all we the rest, although baptized, and born again in Christ, yet

---

[9] This refers to the mediaeval distinction between merit *de congruo* (concerning what is appropriate) and merit *de condigno* (concerning what is wholly deserving). Fallen man was held to be capable of the first by nature and of the second by grace.

[10] Luke 17: 10.

offend in many things; and if we say we have no sin, we deceive ourselves, and the truth is not in us.[11]

16. *Of sin after baptism*

Not every deadly sin willingly committed after baptism is sin against the Holy Ghost, and unpardonable. Wherefore the grant of repentance is not to be denied to such as fall into sin after baptism. After we have received the Holy Ghost, we may depart from grace given, and fall into sin, and by the grace of God we may arise again, and amend our lives. And therefore they are to be condemned, which say, they can no more sin as long as they live here, or deny the place of forgiveness to such as truly repent.

17. *Of predestination and election* [12]

Predestination to life is the everlasting purpose of God, whereby (before the foundations of the world were laid) he hath constantly decreed by his counsel secret to us, to deliver from curse and damnation those whom he hath chosen in Christ out of mankind, and to bring them by Christ to everlasting salvation, as vessels made to honour. Wherefore, they which be endued with so excellent a benefit of God be called according to God's purpose by his Spirit working in due season: they through grace obey the calling: they be Justified freely: they be made sons of God by adoption: they be made like the image of his only-begotten Son Jesus Christ: they walk religiously in good works, and at length, by God's mercy, they attain to everlasting felicity.

As the godly consideration of predestination, and our election in Christ, is full of sweet, pleasant, and unspeakable comfort to godly persons, and such as feel in themselves the working of the Spirit of Christ, mortifying the works of the flesh, and their earthly members, and drawing up their mind to high and heavenly things, as well because it doth greatly establish and confirm their faith of eternal salvation to be enjoyed through Christ, as because it doth fervently kindle their love towards God:

---

[11] The references are to John 1:29; 1 Peter 1:19; 1 John 3:5; 1 John 1:8.
[12] 'election' means 'choice', in this case made by God.

So, for curious[13] and carnal persons, lacking the Spirit of Christ, to have continually before their eyes the sentence of God's predestination, is a most dangerous down-fall, whereby the Devil doth thrust them either into desperation, or into wretchlessness of most unclean living, no less perilous than desperation.

Furthermore, we must receive God's promises in such wise, as they be generally set forth to us in holy Scripture: and, in our doings, that will of God is to be followed, which we have expressly declared unto us in the Word of God.

18. *Of obtaining eternal salvation only by the name of Christ*

They also are to be had accursed that presume to say, That every man shall be saved by the law or sect which he professeth, so that he be diligent to frame his life according to that law, and the light of nature. For holy Scripture doth set out unto us only the name of Jesus Christ, whereby men must be saved.[14]

19. *Of the Church*

The visible Church of Christ is a congregation of faithful men,[15] in the which the pure Word of God is preached, and the sacraments be duly ministered according to Christ's ordinance in all those things that of necessity are requisite to the same.

As the Church of Jerusalem, Alexandria, and Antioch, have erred; so also the Church of Rome hath erred, not only in their living and manner of ceremonies, but also in matters of faith.

20. *Of the authority of the Church*

The Church hath power to decree rites or ceremonies,[16] and authority in controversies of faith: and yet it is not lawful for the Church to ordain any thing that is contrary to God's Word

---

[13] 'curious' is used in the old (and bad) sense of 'prying', 'unduly inquisitive'.

[14] Acts 4: 12

[15] 'faithful' in old English has its etymological sense of 'full of faith', 'believing'.

[16] 'rites or ceremonies' is probably used here in a broad sense, to include forms of service. Compare Article 34, where 'ceremonies or rites' is used interchangeably with 'traditions and ceremonies', and Article 19.

written, neither may it so expound one place of Scripture, that it be repugnant to another. Wherefore, although the Church be a witness and a keeper of holy Writ, yet, as it ought not to decree any thing against the same, so besides the same ought it not to enforce any thing to be believed for necessity of salvation.

21. *Of the authority of general councils*

General councils may not be gathered together without the commandment and will of princes. And when they be gathered together, (forasmuch as they be an assembly of men, whereof all be not governed with the Spirit and Word of God,) they may err, and sometimes have erred, even in things pertaining unto God. Wherefore things ordained by them as necessary to salvation have neither strength nor authority, unless it may be declared that they be taken out of holy Scripture.

22. *Of purgatory* [17]

The Romish doctrine concerning purgatory, pardons, worshipping and adoration, as well of images as of reliques, and also invocation of saints, is a fond thing vainly invented, and grounded upon no warranty of Scripture, but rather repugnant to the Word of God.

23. *Of ministering in the congregation*

It is not lawful for any man to take upon him the office of publick preaching, or ministering the sacraments in the congregation, before he be lawfully called, and sent to execute the same. And

---

[17] 'Purgatory' means 'place of cleansing'. It is a speculation of the late patristic period, and refers to a supposed third state in the life to come, a place of suffering in which souls who die in a state of grace and are ultimately destined for heaven still have to payoff the temporal punishment of their mortal sins for a longer or shorter period. 'Pardons' (Latin *indulgentiae*) means the remission of part of the time a soul has to spend in purgatory, which the papacy claimed to be able to dispense. The sale of pardons, or indulgences, for money was one of the precipitating causes of the Reformation. 'Invocation of saints' means 'calling upon the saints', ie. directing requests to them in the manner of prayers.

those we ought to judge lawfully called and sent, which be chosen and called to this work by men who have publick authority given unto them in the congregation, to call and send ministers into the Lord's vineyard.

24. *Of speaking in the congregation in such a tongue as the people understand*

It is a thing plainly repugnant to the Word of God, and the custom of the primitive Church, to have publick prayer in the Church, or to minister the sacraments in a tongue not understanded of the people.

25. *Of the sacraments*

Sacraments ordained of Christ be not only badges or tokens of Christian men's profession, but rather they be certain sure witnesses, and effectual signs of grace, and God's good will towards us, by the which he doth work invisibly in us, and doth not only quicken, but also strengthen and confirm our faith in him.

There are two sacraments ordained of Christ our Lord in the Gospel, that is to say, baptism, and the supper of the Lord.

Those five commonly called sacraments, that is to say, confirmation, penance, orders, matrimony, and extreme unction[18] are not to be counted for sacraments of the Gospel, being such as have grown partly of the corrupt following of the Apostles, partly are states of life allowed in the Scriptures; but yet have not like nature of sacraments with baptism and the Lord's Supper, for that they have not any visible sign or ceremony ordained of God.

The sacraments were not ordained of Christ to be gazed upon, or to be carried about, but that we should duly use them. And in such only as worthily receive the same they have a wholesome effect or operation: but they that receive them unworthily

---

[18] 'extreme unction' means 'anointing at the end of life'. The ancient anointing of the sick, primarily for their bodily healing and in the expectation of their recovery, was changed in the middle ages into an anointing purely for the benefit of their soul, when all expectation of their recovery had been abandoned.

purchase to themselves damnation, as Saint Paul saith.[19]

26. *Of the unworthiness of the ministers, which hinders not the effect of the sacrament*

Although in the visible Church the evil be ever mingled with the good, and sometimes the evil have chief authority in the ministration of the Word and sacraments, yet forasmuch as they do not the same in their own name, but in Christ's, and do minister by his commission and authority, we may use their ministry, both in hearing the Word of God, and in receiving of the sacraments. Neither is the effect of Christ's ordinance taken away by their wickedness, nor the grace of God's gifts diminished from such as by faith and rightly do receive the sacraments ministered unto them; which be effectual, because of Christ's institution and promise, although they be ministered by evil men.

Nevertheless, it appertaineth to the discipline of the Church, that enquiry be made of evil ministers, and that they be accused by those that have knowledge of their offences; and finally being found guilty, by just judgement be deposed.

27. *Of baptism*

Baptism is not only a sign of profession, and mark of difference, whereby Christian men are discerned from others that be not christened, but it is also a sign of regeneration or new birth, whereby, as by an instrument,[20] they that receive baptism rightly are grafted into the Church; the promises of forgiveness of sin, and of our adoption to be the sons of God by the Holy Ghost, are visibly signed and sealed; faith is confirmed, and grace increased by virtue of prayer unto God. The baptism of young children is in any wise to be retained in the Church, as most agreeable with the institution of Christ.

---

[19] 'damnation' is old English for 'condemnation'. The reference is to 1 Corinthians 11:27-32
[20] 'instrument' (Latin *instrumentum*) may mean a legal instrument, though the verb 'grafted' is rather against this.   If not, the stress of the Article will be on 'rightly' (Latin *recte*), since this too makes the effect of baptism conditional.

28. *Of the Lord's Supper*

The Supper of the Lord is not only a sign of the love that Christians ought to have among themselves one to another; but rather is a sacrament of our redemption by Christ's death: insomuch that to such as rightly, worthily, and with faith, receive the same, the bread which we break is a partaking of the Body of Christ; and likewise the cup of blessing is a partaking of the Blood of Christ.

Transubstantiation (or the change of the substance of bread and wine) in the Supper of the Lord, cannot be proved by holy Writ; but is repugnant to the plain words of Scripture, overthroweth the nature of a sacrament, and hath given occasion to many superstitions.

The Body of Christ is given, taken, and eaten, in the Supper, only after an heavenly and spiritual manner. And the mean whereby the Body of Christ is received and eaten in the Supper is faith.

The sacrament of the Lord's Supper was not by Christ's ordinance reserved, carried about, lifted up, or worshipped.

29. *Of the wicked which eat not the Body of Christ in the use of the Lord's Supper*

The wicked, and such as be void of a lively faith, although they do carnally and visibly press with their teeth (as Saint Augustine saith) the sacrament of the Body and Blood of Christ, yet in no wise are they partakers of Christ: but rather, to their condemnation, do eat and drink the sign or sacrament of so great a thing.

30. *Of both kinds*

The cup of the Lord is not to be denied to the lay-people: for both the parts of the Lord's sacrament, by Christ's ordinance and commandment, ought to be ministered to all Christian men alike.

31. *Of the one oblation of Christ finished upon the Cross*

The offering of Christ once made is that perfect redemption, propitiation, and satisfaction, for all the sins of the whole world, both original and actual; and there is none other satisfaction for sin, but that alone. Wherefore the sacrifices of masses, in the which it was commonly said, that the priest did offer Christ for the quick and the dead, to have remission of pain or guilt, were blasphemous fables, and dangerous deceits.

32. *Of the marriage of priests*

Bishops, priests, and deacons, are not commanded by God's Law, either to vow the estate of single life, or to abstain from marriage: therefore it is lawful for them, as for all other Christian men, to marry at their own discretion, as they shall judge the same to serve better to godliness.

33. *Of excommunicate persons, how they are to be avoided*

That person which by open denunciation of the Church is rightly cut off from the unity of the Church, and excommunicated, ought to be taken of the whole multitude of the faithful, as an heathen and publican,[21] until he be openly reconciled by penance, and received into the Church by a judge that hath authority thereunto.

34. *Of the traditions of the Church*

It is not necessary that traditions and ceremonies be in all places one, and utterly like; for at all times they have been divers, and may be changed according to the diversities of countries, times, and men's manners, so that nothing be ordained against God's Word. Whosoever through his private judgement, willingly and purposely, doth openly break the traditions and ceremonies of the Church, which be not repugnant to the Word of God, and be ordained and approved by common authority, ought to be rebuked openly, (that others may fear to do the like,) as he that offendeth against the common order of the Church, and hurteth the authority of the magistrate, and woundeth the consciences of the weak brethren.

Every particular or national Church hath authority to ordain,

---

[21] The reference is to Matthew 18: 17. A 'publican', of course, was a tax-collector.

change, and abolish, ceremonies or rites of the Church ordained only by man's authority, so that all things be done to edifying.

35. *Of the homilies*

The second book of homilies, the several titles whereof we have joined under this Article, doth contain a godly and wholesome doctrine, and necessary for these times, as doth the former book of homilies, which were set forth in the time of Edward the Sixth; and therefore we judge them to be read in Churches by the ministers, diligently and distinctly, that they may be understanded of the people.[22]

Of the names of the homilies

1. Of the right use of the Church
2. Against peril of idolatry
3. Of repairing and keeping clean of Churches
4. Of good works: first of fasting
5. Against gluttony and drunkenness
6. Against excess of apparel
7. Of prayer
8. Of the place and time of prayer
9. That common prayers and sacraments ought to be ministered in a known tongue
10. Of the reverend estimation of God's Word
11. Of alms-doing
12. Of the nativity of Christ
13. Of the Passion of Christ
14. Of the Resurrection of Christ
15. Of the worthy receiving of the sacrament of the Body and Blood of Christ
16. Of the gifts of the Holy Ghost
17. For the rogation-days
18. Of the state of matrimony
19. Of repentance
20. Against idleness
21. Against rebellion

36. *Of consecration of bishops and ministers*

The Book of Consecration of archbishops and bishops, and

---

[22] The *Book of Homilies* is in fact two books of Homilies, but after Elizabeth's reign they were always bound up together.

ordering of priests and deacons, lately set forth in the time of Edward the Sixth, and confirmed at the same time by authority of Parliament, doth contain all things necessary to such consecration and ordering: neither hath it any thing, that of itself is superstitious and ungodly. And therefore whosoever are consecrated or ordered according to the rites of that Book, since the second year of the forenamed King Edward unto this time, or hereafter shall be consecrated or ordered according to the same rites; we decree all such to be rightly, orderly, and lawfully consecrated and ordered.

37. *Of the civil magistrates*

The King's Majesty hath the chief power in this realm of England, and other his dominions, unto whom the chief government of all estates of this realm, whether they be ecclesiastical or civil, in all causes doth appertain, and is not, nor ought to be, subject to any foreign jurisdiction.

Where we attribute to the King's Majesty the chief government, by which titles we understand the minds of some slanderous folks to be offended; we give not to our princes the ministering either of God's Word, or of the sacraments, the which thing the injunctions also lately set forth by Elizabeth our Queen do most plainly testify; but that only prerogative, which we see to have been given always to all godly princes in holy Scriptures by God himself; that is, that they should rule all estates and degrees committed to their charge by God, whether they be ecclesiastical or temporal, and restrain with the civil sword the stubborn and evildoers.

The bishop of Rome hath no jurisdiction in this realm of England.

The laws of the realm may punish Christian men with death, for heinous and grievous offences.

It is lawful for Christian men, at the commandment of the magistrate, to wear weapons, and serve in the wars.

38. *Of Christian men's goods, which are not common*

The riches and goods of Christians are not common, as touching the right, title, and possession of the same, as certain anabaptists do falsely boast. Notwithstanding, every man ought, of such things as he possesseth, liberally to give alms to the poor, according to his ability.

39. *Of a Christian man's oath*

As we confess that vain and rash swearing is forbidden Christian men by our Lord Jesus Christ, and James his apostle, so we judge, that Christian religion doth not prohibit, but that a man may swear when the magistrate requireth, in a cause of faith and charity, so it be done according to the prophet's teaching, in justice, judgement, and truth.[23]

THE RATIFICATION

This Book of Articles before rehearsed, is again approved, and allowed to be holden and executed within the realm, by the assent and consent of our Sovereign Lady ELIZABETH, by the grace of God, of England, France, and Ireland, Queen, Defender of the Faith, &c. Which Articles were deliberately read, and confirmed again by the subscription of the hands of the archbishop and bishops of the upper-house, and by the subscription of the whole clergy of the nether-house in their Convocation, in the Year of our Lord 1571.

---

[23] The references are to Matthew 5:33-37; James 5:12; Jeremiah 4:2.

I. INTRODUCTION

WHEN I look back on my 27 years of ordained service in the Church of England and ask myself what I was up to during that time, the answer that comes is this. I sought two goals, which in a sense were one, since the latter was a means to the former. First, having been converted at university out of the formalist folk religion that passed for Anglicanism where I was brought up, I longed to see English parishes come evangelically alive, and I worked to that end throughout. But, second, having met the Church of England's Reformed and Puritan heritage in the writings of such men as J. C. Ryle, I saw that the healthiest discipleship, the truest maturity, the worthiest worship and the weightiest witness flow from deep acquaintance with God's revealed truth, deeper than was generally sought in the circles I knew. So I with others campaigned specifically for more study of the biblical faith, more use of the mind in loving God, more theological alertness among Anglican evangelicals generally. We hoped to further both reformation and revival through letting God's word loose in this way.

For over a decade up to about 1965 I thought that in theological education, parish programmes, clergy vision and lay interest, significant ground was being gained. Since then, however, my impression is that due to a combination of factors, some distracting and some opposing, anti-intellectual pietism, fed and watered by the book trade, has largely regained control. Bible study remains, and books for the purpose with titles like *Food for Life* abound; evangelism and nurture remain, and books with titles like *Discipleship* abound also; but theological concern – by which I mean, the passion to know everything coherently and thoroughly in terms of God's word, will and work – has ebbed. The one area of exception here is social standards, where ethical insight – ethics is, of course, a branch of theology – seems to have deepened steadily, at least on some issues.

However, I see big differences between the Anglican pietism of the first half of this century and that of the second. The former was rigid and prickly in maintaining Protestant churchmanship, seeing this as an important way of protesting against unevangelical doctrine. Also, it kept its distance from the Church's centralized institutional life, in protest against worldly and self-seeking things that seemed to go on there. Today's pietism, however, tends to treat 'Protestant' as a dirty word, to ignore the distinctives of Protestant churchmanship, and to involve itself heavily in diocesan and synodical affairs, sometimes appearing to crave recognition more than it desires reformation. Evangelicals have 'made their contribution' (the phrase is in quotes because it has gained almost shibboleth status) to England's obstinately Broad Church establishment in a way that would once have been thought impossible for them, on conscientious grounds. I hope I am wrong to suspect that with this enhanced participation has come a lessening of theological seriousness; for if I am right, then how ever evangelical numbers grow (and numerical growth since 1950 has been spectacular) evangelical thought will hardly be able to maintain its own integrity, let alone shape the future outlook of the Church of England. But, though I wish to be wrong, I cannot yet persuade myself that I am.

For the past two centuries two ingredients have mixed to form Anglican evangelicalism, mixing in different proportions in different men. One ingredient has been the theologically vigorous anti-Roman national-church outlook of such as Jewel, Hooker, Pearson, Waterland, and more recently William Goode, Hugh McNeile, Nathaniel Dimock, Henry Wace, E. A. Knox, Daniel Bartlett, Charles Sydney Carter and many others. The second ingredient is this generally pacific pietism which stemmed from the evangelical revival of the eighteenth century and centred its concern on personal conversion, 'serious' living, disciplined devotion, edifying conversation, good causes, and soul-winning at home and abroad. The Clapham Sect, Charles Simeon and Handley C. G. Moule exemplify it. When the two ingredients have blended in equal strength in capacious minds, the result has been impressive: J. C. Ryle, T. P. Boultbee, W. H. Griffith Thomas, T. C. Hammond, A. M. Stibbs are instances. In smaller, narrower minds, however, whichever interest dominates has tended always to mute the other, producing lopsidedness – either a clear-headed, sharp-tongued, and sometimes cold-hearted Protestantism, or else devotional warmth in a haze of doctrinal woolliness. Currently, as I said above, I judge that pacific pietism is very much on top, and though many pietists know the historical theology of Reformation debate well, few seem able to see what Reformation principles imply for Anglican churches today.

I write the present essay because I believe that facing and dialoguing with the Thirty-nine Articles will help Anglicans both to re-learn and to re-apply some basic biblical truths with which authentic Anglican identity is bound up. Not only will this exercise give evangelical pietism its needed theological stuffing; it will also have the effect of drawing all Anglicans closer to Christ, and so to each other. With the modern idea that it would be safest, wisest and healthiest to forget about the Articles altogether I disagree profoundly.

I believe that in a divided Christendom churches need confessional statements, and that it is always unrealistic to try to do without them. I believe that good creedal and confessional formulations always in any case have a major role to play in educating and maturing the people of God. I believe that the domestic statements of faith that emerged all over Western Europe at the time of the Reformation, the Thirty-nine Articles among them, have great theological strength and value, and are permanently important in the ecumenical quest for the unity of the faith. I further believe that churches ought to keep in touch with their doctrinal bases, valuing them as confessions of faith and challenges to faithfulness rather than dismissing them as phrased curiosities. With scholars generally, I believe that the Anglican Articles are a skilfully framed, high-quality domestic creed. With Anglican evangelicals generally, I believe that their account of Christian basics is biblical, true and essential. I hope that the course of my argument will justify all these convictions, which I state now so that the reader may know my standpoint. I think that the whole Church of England today would be immeasurably enriched by a renewing of serious encounter with its own Articles, and none will be happier than I if what I write helps to bring this about.

2.   THE SILENCE OF THE ARTICLES

'WHAT shall we do with the drunken sailor?' asks the capstan-pushers' work-song. Is there not need to ask a parallel question about the Church of England? Not that one could call so staid a body drunken, exactly; but there are aspects of churchly sobriety which Anglicans in England (to look no further) have largely neglected for a long time. One of these is the maintaining of a responsible relationship to the Thirty-nine Articles. The work-song makes its picturesque proposals for getting the drunken sailor sober again, and I have some sobering suggestions to make about links with the Articles which we urgently need to set up. But first we must take a long, hard look at things as they are.

The Articles were drawn up more than four centuries ago to be a statement of the Church's position on many key questions and thus an abiding test of soundness for the clergy, who would all be required to subscribe them.   As an official presentation of Anglican orthodoxy, they were seen as fit material for instructing layfolk, and prior to this century were often used in that way. Today, however, Anglican laymen neither know nor care about the Articles; talks are not given on them, books are not written about them, theologians ignore them, and most clergy, though they have subscribed them, would have to admit if asked that they habitually evade at least some of them. Sometimes they are quoted for ridicule, either because their wording sounds quaint or because what they say is thought old-fashioned to the point of weirdness. ('Fancy! The Articles say that God is without parts or passions! that Jesus died to reconcile his Father to us! that his risen body had bones! that the Pelagians do vainly talk! that Purgatory is a fond thing vainly invented! What funny old stuff!' etc.). More often, however, like sleeping dogs, the Articles are simply left to lie, and the Church carries on as if they had never existed.

2.1. The Articles have no voice in Anglican Theology

So they have no voice in contemporary Anglican *theology*. If they are referred to at all in theological colleges, it is as historical memorials, not as bulwarks of Anglican faith or challenges to our present-day waywardness. Today's Anglican theologians embrace all sorts of notions, but they do not speak as men who have seriously grappled with the witness of the Articles on any subject at all; and the harmonious soundness of teaching which clerical assent was meant to ensure never seems to materialize. This was already a long-standing problem in 1939. In that year the then Bishop of Durham, Herbert Hensley Henson, wrote about it as follows.

> The *raison d'etre* of subscription to the Thirty-nine Articles is the necessity, in a divided Christendom, of agreeing on a version of the Catholic Faith. In the Articles we have the Anglican version of the Catholic tradition of Faith and Discipline. It is not open to any loyal Anglican to form any other.

> Alike for negotiations with other branches of the Church, and for the instruction of its own members, *some* authoritative statement of specifically Anglican teaching and practice is really indispensable. Such an authoritative statement is provided by the Thirty-nine Articles, and, if they were abandoned, it would be necessary to provide a substitute.

> So long as the Christian society is divided on issues so fundamental as to transcend even the interest of visible unity, separate Churches must exist, and must show cause for doing so. It would be manifestly intolerable that men should be authorized to minister as officers and teachers who did not assent to the doctrine and discipline of the Church which commissioned them. It would be not less intolerable if the parishioners were to possess no security against mere individualism on the part of the clergy. Therefore it seems to follow that Subscription is really indispensable, as well for the protection of the people as for the security of the Church.

> When, however, we pass from theoretical considerations to the actual situation in the Church of England at the present time, we are confronted by a strange spectacle of doctrinal confusion which demonstrates the failure of Subscription to secure either of

the two objects for which presumably it was designed. It does not provide any effective guarantee of the doctrinal soundness of the subscribing clergy, and it does not protect the people from heretical parsons. The Church of England, at the present time, exhibits a doctrinal incoherence which has no parallel in any other church claiming to be traditionally orthodox.[1]

It would take a bold man to argue that Henson's words have ceased to apply since the day when he wrote them. The only change there seems to have been is that the clergyman's temptation to treat the Articles as a dead letter has become stronger than ever, because of the way that ordinands are nowadays taught theology. Anglican textbooks of theology used to take the form of discursive expositions of the Articles, those by Bicknell (liberal Catholic) and Griffith Thomas (evangelical Protestant) being the ones most widely used.[2] (The last in that line was *Anglican Teaching* by Wilson and Templeton, two learned Irishmen, published in 1962.[3]) But today the commonest textbook is John Macquarrie's *Principles of Christian Theology* (1967; second edition 1977), a work by an Anglican which never mentions the Articles, and I know of no University faculty or theological college where theology is taught in dialogical relation to the Articles in the older fashion. I do not suggest that the more ecumenical scope and style of modern Anglican clergy education is a total disaster; I merely observe that, whatever else may be said for it, it is calculated to ensure that the Articles will never shape Anglican theology again.

---

[1] Herbert Hensley Henson, *The Church of England*, (Cambridge: CUP, 1939), pp. 107f.

[2] E. J. Bicknell, *A Theological Introduction to the Thirty-nine Articles of the Church of England*, (London: Longmans, Green, 1919; third edition, revised and with bibliography by H. J. Carpenter, 1955); W. H. Griffith Thomas, *The Principles of Theology: An Introduction to the Thirty-nine Articles*, (London: Church Book Room Press, 1930; new edition, with introduction and bibliography by J. I. Packer, 1977.)

[3] W. G. Wilson and J. H. Templeton, *Anglican Teaching : An Exposition of the Thirty-nine Articles* (Dublin APCK, 1962.) The most recent brief exposition was David Broughton Knox, *Thirty-nine Articles: The Historic Basis of Anglican Faith* (London: Hodder and Stoughton, 1967.)

2.2.   The Articles have no voice in Anglican Liturgy

Moreover, the Articles have no voice in contemporary Anglican *liturgy*. Historically, it has long been understood that the Articles formulate the beliefs which the Prayer Book services express, and in terms of which those services ought now to be interpreted. By parity of reasoning, therefore, the Articles relate in the same way to the various revised and/or newly devised worship forms (it is sometimes hard to know which description fits) that the Anglican communion has produced in recent years. Or do they? It is plain that the framers of these forms rarely thought in these terms, if indeed they did so at any point at all. Comparing the new services is a fascinating study.[4] The powerful pressure towards standardization which today affects all manufacturers of anything has clearly been felt by Anglican liturgy-makers worldwide. Liturgical commissions in different provinces have had access to each other's work, and borrowed from it, and we can fairly say that we are seeing the fulfilment of the hope expressed at the 1958 Lambeth Conference,

> that it is now possible to work towards a liturgy which will win its way throughout the Anglican Communion ... a basic pattern for the service of Holy Communion which will commend itself to all provinces.[5]

But, just as the authors of the baptismal rites in the 1980 *Alternative Service Book* (ASB) showed no interest in expressing liturgically the doctrine of original sin (Articles 9,10), and did not

---

[4] To start this study, see B. J. Wigan, *The Liturgy in English* (London: Alcuin Club. 1962); C. O. Buchanan, *Modern Anglican Liturgies, 1958-1968* (London: OUP, 1968); *Further Anglican Liturgies, 1968-1975* (Bramcote: Grove Books, 1975); G. J. Cuming, *A History of Anglican Liturgy* (London: Macmillan, 1969, second edition 1982); *The Book of Common Prayer* (New York: Church Hymnal Corporation and Seabury Press, 1977); *An Australian Prayer Book* (Sydney: Anglican Information Office Press, 1978); *The Alternative Service Book 1980* (London: SPCK, Clowes, and Cambridge: CUP, 1980.)

[5] *The Lambeth Conference 1958* (London: SPCK and Greenwich: Seabury Press), 2:81.

in fact clearly express it as the 1662 rite did, so the authors of the new Communion services have shown no concern to express liturgically the drama and glory of the sinner's justification by faith only (Articles 10-16) as the 1662 rite, following Cranmer, did, and have in fact, at least by comparison, smudged this theme considerably. One cannot blame modern liturgy-writers for following theological fashion (what else could you ask them to do?); but plainly, to Anglicans who worship in churches where ASB is used more often than 1662, or who simply want to be in step with the Anglican communion as a whole, the status of the Articles as the Church of England's official statement of belief must henceforth seem increasingly anomalous and anachronistic.

2.3. The Articles have no voice in Anglican Community

What I describe is a state of affairs in which the Articles have no real voice in Anglican *community;* not because anyone wishes them harm, but because ordinarily no one thinks about them at all. Not merely are they not the focus of unity within the Anglican communion; they play no effective part in the conception of that unity. Granted, the Lambeth Conference of 1888 laid it down that new missionary churches should be recognized as Anglican only if 'their Clergy subscribe Articles in accordance with the express statements of our standards of doctrine and worship' – though it added that 'they should not necessarily be bound to accept in their entirety the Thirty-nine Articles of Religion.'[6] Fair enough, we may say; the Articles are all sixteenth-century Western Church products, and some relate to Tudor England specifically, and they could hardly make an ideal basis of faith for a new church in, say, Africa or the South Seas.[7] But the positive requirement of this resolution

---

[6] *The Lambeth Conferences, 1867-1930* (London: SPCK, 1948), p. 292.
[7] Yet the first of the Fundamental Provisions of the Constitution of the Church of Uganda states: 'The Church of Uganda doth hold and maintain the doctrines and sacraments of Christ ... as the Church of England hath received the same in the Book of Common Prayer, and in the form and manner of making, ordaining and consecrating of Bishops, Priests, and Deacons and in the Thirty-nine

has in practice been honoured as much in the breach as in the observance.[8] Also, it should be noted that in the constantly affirmed 'Lambeth Quadrilateral' (Scripture, the ecumenical creeds, the two dominical sacraments and the historic episcopate as the Anglican basis for unity) no mention is made of the Articles. And when in 1968 the Articles gained a place on the Lambeth agenda, presumably because of the report *Subscription and Assent to the 39 Articles* which the (English) Archbishops' Doctrine Commission had produced in that year, the discussion was less than positive, as the two references to the Articles in *The Lambeth Conference 1968* show.

The first reference is an Addendum to the committee report on 'Renewal in Faith', headed 'The Thirty-nine Articles and the Anglican Tradition'[9]. It states that assent to the Articles should be understood as 'an expression of a determination to be loyal to our multiple inheritance of faith', which includes more than the Articles. Fair enough, we may again say; all mature churches do in fact operate, and rightly, under 'an authority of a multiple kind' in which Scripture, the witness of the Christian past, and the demand that faith be shown reasonable by the criteria of historicity and coherence, all play a part, alongside any domestic creed that these churches may have. But the Addendum fails to acknowledge either Scripture, the primary standard, or the Articles, the subordinate standard, as having any normative, interpretative, or critical relation to the rest of the 'inheritance of faith' as it has filled out over the years; and, lacking this, the statement that the Articles have 'their place in the historical context of a continuous, developing Anglican tradition'[10] sounds too much like the Roman Catholicism of Cardinal Newman for comfort.

Articles of Religion, and further it disclaims for itself the right of altering any of the aforesaid standards of faith and doctrine.'

[8] See Archbishops' Commission on Christian Doctrine, *Subscription and Assent to the 39 Articles* (London: SPCK, 1968), pp. 19-24, for evidence on this.

[9] *The Lambeth Conference 1968* (London: SPCK and New York: Seabury Press), pp. 82f.

[10] Ibid., p. 82.

The second reference is Resolution 43, which reads thus :

> The Conference accepts the main conclusion of the report *Subscription and Assent* and in furtherance of its recommendation
>
> a. suggests that each Church of our communion consider whether the Articles need be bound up with its Prayer Book;
>
> b. suggests to the Churches of the Anglican Communion that assent to the Thirty-nine Articles be no longer required of ordinands;
>
> c. suggests that, when subscription is required to the Articles or other elements in the Anglican tradition, it should be required, and given, only in the context of a statement which gives the full range of our inheritance of faith and sets the Articles in their historical context.[11]

Now this was a nonsense, worthy perhaps of drunken sailors but hardly of sober bishops. (c) really was in accord with the report's recommendation. On (a) it should be noted that the report recommended retaining the Articles in the Prayer Book,[12] so that '*need*' ought to have read '*should not*' if the furtherance of the report's recommendation had been genuinely in view. But (b) contradicts the report's recommendation directly. The whole resolution was in fact the product of a rushed half-hour's debate carried through in extra time at the end of the Conference's final morning. (b) was an amendment from the floor, accepted on a snap vote. The Chairman of the Archbishops' Doctrine Commission, Bishop Ian Ramsey of Durham, who had introduced the resolution, himself voted against it in its amended form, and later encouraged the Church Assembly to treat the offspring of Lambeth's lapse as a joke rather than a charismatic oracle. But the fact that this could happen at all shows how little concern for the Articles most Anglican bishops can muster in these days.

---

[11] Ibid., pp. 40f.
[12] *Subscription and Assent,* section 100, p. 76.

2.4. Neglecting the Articles creates a Problem of Anglican Integrity

It must by now be clear that the problem of where the Articles fit into the modern Church of England cannot be simply laughed off. It is too serious. It is at heart a problem of *integrity*. On this question, as on others, the Church of England causes real scandal by appearing, Janus-like, to face both ways. We celebrate the Articles without listening to them; we affirm them while stopping our ears to them; we tip our hats to them while we gag them. On the one hand, Canons A2 and A5 of the present code state respectively that

> The Thirty-nine Articles are agreeable to the Word of God and may be assented unto with a good conscience by all members of the Church of England,

and that

> The doctrine of the Church of England is grounded in the Holy Scriptures, and in such teachings of the ancient Fathers and Councils of the Church as are agreeable to the said Scriptures. In particular such doctrine is to be found in the Thirty-nine Articles of Religion, the Book of Common Prayer, and the Ordinal.

On the other hand, no layman is required to subscribe or even to know the Articles; the present form of clerical subscription involves no direct endorsement of any specific thing that the Articles say; and clergymen accused of contradicting the Articles plead guilty without turning a hair – as well they may, for they know they will not be penalized for their position. In plain words, we treat the Articles as a 4000-word historical curio which because of its age is no longer fit to function as the domestic creed and standard that we profess it to be. The question of our integrity then arises in an acute form, because our constitutional entrenching and our practical downgrading of the Articles are so much out of line with each other.

What moves the modern Church of England to treat its Articles so lightly? Various reasons operate for various people, but here I deal with the one that is perhaps the most respectable. The

Church of England claims to be the catholic church of God in England, and the chronic suspicion is that, being a local, polemical and somewhat *ad hoc* product, the Articles are an essentially sectarian document, one which impedes the claim to catholicity rather than supports it. But this idea is wrong-headed, and ironically so, for exactly the reverse is true. Catholicity is a matter of belief and of doctrine before it is anything else, and the Articles contain what the title of Thomas Rogers' augmented exposition of them in 1607 called 'the catholic doctrine believed and professed in the Church of England'. The Articles demonstrate catholicity, not diminish it. Any other view argues a sectarian idea of catholicity itself – sectarian, I mean, in the classic sense of making, or seeing, division where the Lord neither makes nor sees it, and thereby failing to acknowledge and express unity which the Lord has actually established. The Presbyterian A. C. Cochrane writes of the Articles:

> A Reformed Church would surely see in a Church of England professing the Thirty-nine Articles a genuine Evangelical and Protestant Church and (one) which *in this sense* is the one, holy, catholic Church.

> Unfortunately,

(so he continues, with a courteous mildness that is hardly deserved)

> one is never quite sure whether the Church of England herself wishes her catholicity to be understood in terms of the Thirty-nine Articles! [13]

'!' indeed. A less charitable observer would say that the Church of England clearly does *not* wish its catholicity to be understood in these terms; for actions speak louder than words, and Anglican action is in effect a request to others not to take seriously our fine words about the Articles, since we do not take them seriously

---

[13] Arthur C. Cochrane, *Reformed Confessions of the Sixteenth Century* (London: SCM Press, 1966), p. 22

ourselves. Anglicans (so the observer might also say) make a virtue at this point of an attitude to their own public statements which in politics would be called cynical duplicity and in business bad faith. Surely (he might be tempted to add) such an attitude is as unprincipled in the world church as it would be in the political and business worlds, and those who adopt it ought to be ashamed of themselves.

Now this is not a new thought; it is a sentiment that during the past hundred years has often been expressed in as well as outside the Church of England, and many Anglicans have had to get used to shrugging it off. But, one asks, how can responsible people do that? How can anyone who is serious in the service of God regard such duplicity and double-talk as justified? Well, attempts to justify it are certainly made, and here I take note of two of them.

First, it has been argued that the true Anglican vocation is to be a *dialectical* communion, a cockpit of discussion and debate in which three types of theology, Reformational, Romanizing, and radical reformist respectively battle it out, while the institution hospitably holds the ring for them all without committing itself in a decisive way to anyone of them.[14] But this is a rationalization of history which history itself explodes. As the learned Philip Schaff pointed out a century ago,

> Continental historians, both Protestant and Catholic, rank the Church of England among the Reformed Churches as distinct from the Lutheran, and her Articles are found in every collection of Reformed Confessions.

He noticed, indeed, as all students of Anglicanism must do, that

> the theological interpretation of the Articles by English writers has been mostly conducted in a controversial rather than an historical spirit ... Moderate High-Churchmen and Arminians,

---

[14] In *A Kind of Noah's Ark? The Anglican Commitment to Comprehensiveness* (Oxford: Latimer House, 1981), pp. 24-26, I discussed this idea as put forward by E. Amand de Mendieta and the 1948 Lambeth Conference.

who dislike Calvinism, represent them as purely Lutheran (footnote: Archbishop Laurence of Cashel, and Hardwick); Anglo-Catholics and Tractarians, who abhor both Lutheranism and Calvinism, endeavour to conform them as much as possible to the contemporary decrees of the Council of Trent (footnote: Newman, Pusey, Forbes); Calvinistic and evangelical Low-Churchmen find in them substantially their own creed.[15]

But Schaff was able to show that on every point save the shape of the Church-state link and the acceptance of episcopacy (Articles 37, 36) the Articles are unambiguously in the Reformed mainstream.[16] The truth is that for over four centuries the Reformed commitment of the Church of England, set forth in the Articles, has been a matter of public fact, and the latter-day suggestion of an essentially dialectical identity for Anglicanism must be dismissed as a private fancy – wishful thinking, without historical warrant, and flying in the face of established historical realities. As I with my British passport cannot convincingly pretend to be a citizen of Bolivia or Brazil at a time of passport inspection, so one cannot convincingly deny the Reformed commitment of the Church of England when the official formularies are taken note of; for one cannot pretend that the Articles do not exist, or are not in fact what they are.

Second, it has been claimed that the Anglicanism of the

---

[15] Philip Schaff, *A History of the Creeds of Christendom* (London: Hodder and Stoughton, 1877), p. 622.

[16] Ibid., pp. 622f. Schaff formulates his conclusion thus: the Articles are catholic on the Trinity and the Incarnation, borrowing phrases from the Lutheran confessions of Augsburg (1530) and Wurtemberg (1552); they are Augustinian, as are all the early Lutheran and Reformed statements on freewill, sin and grace; they are Protestant and evangelical, with all other Reformation confessions, on Scripture, justification, faith and good works, and the church; they are *'Reformed* and *moderately Calvinistic'* on predestination and the Lord's Supper, against the Lutherans; they are Erastian on the royal supremacy in ecclesiastical matters; and they are 'purely Anglican' on bishops. Schaff quotes the letter from Bishop John Jewel, 'the final reviser' of the Articles, to Peter Martyr at Zurich in 1562: 'As to matters of doctrine, we have pared everything away to the very quick, and do not differ from you by a nail's breadth' (p. 603, citing from *Zurich Letters* [London: Parker Society (P.S.), 1842] 1.100).

Church of England since the Reformation should be defined in *liturgical* terms only. An oracular editorial in *The Times* on January 19th, 1960, said:

> to hold that (what Christians believe) is better expressed in the forms of corporate worship than in theological definitions ... It is the Book of Common Prayer ... and not the Articles, in which Anglicanism consists.

Really? Is Anglicanism, then, just a liturgical ethos as distinct from a confessional position? Is the title-deed of the Church of England just a set of statutory services apart from any statement of faith? Cranmer, and Laud, and the latitudinarian Burnet, and the eighteenth and nineteenth century Evangelicals, and the Tractarians, and Pusey, and the judges who gave verdicts in the heresy and ritual trials of the last century, and indeed the whole history of the post-Reformation Church of England till this century, will tell us, if we let them speak. Historic Anglicanism is not just a style of worship; it is also, and fundamentally, a confessional stance. The idea that the essence of Anglicanism is the Prayer Book without the Articles is another twentieth-century rationalisation of history – a further private fancy, spun out of the fact that folk who thought (not always correctly) that they had completely different theologies have yet been able to use the same forms of public prayer.

It is, of course, open to anyone to argue that Anglicanism needs redefining in our day, just as it needed redefining in the sixteenth century, and that the needed redefinition calls for a change of conviction and course now as it did then, and that the voice of history and the witness of yesterday ought not to limit what Anglicanism should seek to be today and tomorrow. Such arguments, however, will only have the status of private opinions challenging history; they cannot be represented as the verdict, lesson and message of that history. For Anglican history exhibits a definite theological identity, embodying the recovered catholicity of Protestant evangelical belief, an identity which for three centuries after the Reformation satisfied and even delighted clergy and laity alike, including many who disliked Anglican discipline. When Tractarian and Anglo-Catholic ideologists got down to their self-appointed task of trying to change this identity, party spirit and domestic conflict grew so strong that satisfaction and delight were drastically diminished for everybody, and for that reason among others the Church of England has been a distinctly unhappy church for a century and a half, with an identity problem gnawing at its vitals.   But it does not follow that the Church of England ought now to deny, or forget, the public identity that it has had for almost half a millennium.   There are other and better ways of responding to our situation.

At this point sentimental love for the Church of England as an institution, and triumphalist confidence that whatever is in Anglican life is right, and is blessed by God, sometimes combine to produce genuinely crooked thinking.   It is not crooked thinking to dismiss the Articles as inept, crude, unreflective, sectarian, and unworthy to be a church creed: that is straightforward theological ignorance, which is curable by study and knowledge. Nor is it crooked thinking to peddle a new definition of Anglicanism to any-one who cares to buy it: that is straightforward individualism, the willingness to go out on a limb and look eccentric in what seems a good cause, which is a characteristically English trait, familiar in English society just as it is in English novels.   But it is crooked thinking when the case for redefining Anglicanism is presented as the verdict of Anglican history. It is no such thing; it is a consequence of one's personal theology, one's own (by Anglican standards, eccentric) view as to what Christianity is and isn't, in the light of which one reviews and edits Anglican past history. Our integrity as Anglicans will always be open to question until we are honest enough to face this, and come clean about it.

But in any case, just as it is open to anyone to argue that a new concept of Anglicanism is needed, so it is open to anyone to argue that that is not so at all, and that our real need, for integrity, for unity and for spiritual health, is to lay hold afresh of the old concept from which we have drifted through pursuing party squabbles or trying to patch up party peace; to grasp again the breadth of that old concept, of which the party war has caused many to lose sight; and to deepen it in face of the vast complex of relativist and pluralist theologies which have bubbled up in academia, overflowed into theological education, and largely swamped German- and English-speaking churches worldwide, during the past few decades. That is the thrust of my argument in this essay; and integral to our task (so I shall claim) is a reinstating of the Articles, not only as a standard of belief on specific doctrines, but also as a model of theological method, a challenge to confess the faith of the gospel today, and a constant partner in the Church's theological life. It is my firm conviction that the Articles are true enough, profound enough, biblical enough, evangelical enough, and magisterial enough to sustain such a role amid the babel and bustle of present-day theological work, and that we greatly need to have them fulfilling it among us. They have been silent too long.

3. THE HISTORY OF THE ARTICLES

The purpose of this present discussion, as has already been said, is theological and (if I dare use the word) existential, rather than constitutional or historical, for my concern is not so much with what the status of the Thirty-nine Articles has been in the past as with what it should be now and in the future. But this problem confronts us in a form that has been determined by four centuries of Anglican history, and we cannot hope to resolve it without some knowledge of that history. So my next step will be a fairly full historical retrospect.

For our present purpose, the important facts in the history of the Articles may be set out under four heads.

3.1. *The Establishing of the Articles as a Doctrinal Standard*

The need for positive statements showing where the Church of England stood with reference to the theological disputes of the Reformation was felt within two years of Henry's breach with Rome in 1534. To meet it, the conservative *Ten Articles* were produced in 1536, followed by the more positively Protestant *Institution of a Christian Man* (the 'Bishops' Book', 1537) and the reactionary substitute for it, *A Necessary Doctrine and Erudition for any Christian Man* (the 'King's Book', 1543), each representing different degrees of concession and resistance to the Lutheranism of the Augsburg Confession.[1] When Henry died in 1547, Cranmer, who had long been convinced that on all questions except the eucharistic presence the Lutheran position was both biblical and patristic, set himself to re-cast the entire outward form of the

---

[1] The nearest approach of all to the Augsburg Confession appears in the Thirteen Articles, drawn up in consultation with a Lutheran deputation in 1538, but not published till the nineteenth century. See B. J. Kidd, *Thirty-nine Articles* (London: Rivingtons, 5th edition, 1911), pp. 22f.

Church of England in a reformed mould. Aided by a team of talented theologians, he compiled in quick succession a volume of standard evangelical sermons (the Homilies, 1547); a new Prayer Book and Ordinal (1549 and 1550 respectively; both revised in 1552); a code of canons (1552; published posthumously by John Foxe, the martyrologist, under the title *Reformatio Legum Ecclesiasticarum* in 1571); and, last but not least, the Forty-two Articles of 1553.

This set of cautionary and controversial statements on disputed issues was drawn up at a time of extreme religious confusion. The English clergy were as a body very ignorant, as episcopal visitations like Hooper's had shown; those of them who were capable of understanding the Reformation controversies were sharply divided; and meanwhile Anabaptist vagaries – rationalist, mystical, antinomian – were, or were feared to be, flooding the country. Cranmer's first object in compiling his Articles was that they should establish in this situation a necessary minimum of doctrinal order, by fixing the bounds of belief permissible to Anglican clergy. To safeguard doctrinal truth and order by requiring the clergy to subscribe to orthodox formulae was a practice dating back to the Arian controversy, and one which had already been revived in the churches of the continental Reformation. Cranmer, on his own initiative, it would seem, had adopted this practice as early as 1549, for on December 27th of that year Hooper wrote to Bullinger that

> he [Cranmer] has some articles of religion, to which all preachers and lecturers in divinity are required to subscribe, or else a license for teaching is not granted them.[2]

---

[2] *Original Letters* (Parker Society, 1846), I. 71; cf. p. 76. As Bishop of Gloucester, Hooper himself, 'knowing that many of his clergy were extremely ignorant, and moreover hostile to the Reformation ... drew up a body of fifty articles, to which he required them to subscribe' (*Later Writings of Bishop Hooper* [P.S., 1852], p. xvii; text of articles, pp. 120-9). On July 6, 1552, he wrote to Sir William Cecil: 'For the love of God, cause the Articles that the king's majesty spake of when we took our oaths' – ie, presumably, the coming Forty-two – 'to be set forth by his

It is generally thought that these articles were an early draft of the Forty-two. However that may be, when on November 24th, 1552, Cranmer returned the Forty-two to the Privy Council in their final form, he urged the Councillors in his covering letter

> to be means unto the King's majesty, that all the bishops may have authority from him to cause all their preachers, archdeacons, deans, prebendaries, parsons, vicars, curates with all their clergy, to subscribe to the said Articles. And then I trust that such a concord and quietness in religion shall shortly follow thereof, as else it is not to be looked for many years. God shall thereby be glorified, His truth shall be advanced...[3]

The Forty-two Articles appeared in print in June of the following year, and on the 19th of the month a royal proclamation was issued requiring subscription to them from all clergy, schoolmasters, and members of the Universities. On July 6th, however, less than three weeks later, the King died, and the accession of Mary brought the new order to an abrupt end. But in 1571 both Parliament and Convocation made subscription to the revised version of Cranmer's Articles (the present Thirty-nine) mandatory for ministers, and so it has remained ever since.[4] Canon 36 of 1604 endorsed the form of subscription first set out in Whitgift's Three Articles of 1584, whereby at ordination and each entry upon a new benefice a man had to subscribe 'willingly and *ex*

---

authority ... I will cause every minister to confess them openly before their parishioners...' (p. xviii).

[3] Cranmer, *Miscellaneous Writings* (P.S., 1846), pp. 440f.

[4] The Act of Parliament (13 Eliz.) required subscription to 'all the Articles of Religion, which only concern the confession of the true Christian Faith, and the doctrine of the Sacraments'. The 'only' appears to show that the Puritan laymen who pushed the Bill in Parliament did not mean to compel Puritan clergy to subscribe the Articles relating to the Church's domestic discipline. Also, the Act related to the Articles as published in 1563, ie. without Article 29. But the Convocation of 1571 passed a supplementary provision requiring subscription to all Thirty-nine, and it was this comprehensive subscription that the Court of High Commission began at once to enforce, with the result that about a hundred Puritan clergy were deprived of their livings for non-subscription within a very few months.

animo' to (1) the royal supremacy in church matters, (2) the Prayer Book and Ordinal as containing 'nothing contrary to the word of God', and (3) 'all and every the Articles ... being in number nine and thirty, besides the ratification' as being 'agreeable to the word of God.' Canon 5 of the same code forbade public dissent from the Articles:

> Whosoever shall hereafter affirm, That any of the nine and thirty Articles ... are in any part superstitious or erroneous or such that he may not with good conscience subscribe unto; let him be excommunicated *ipso facto* and not restored, but only by the archbishop, after his repentance, and public revocation of such his wicked errors.

Thus the Articles became the authorized doctrinal standard of the Church of England: terms of communion for the laity, who were forbidden to speak against them, and a confession of faith for the clergy, who were obliged to subscribe them. As Dr. Routley rightly says: 'the Articles are designed to be the Rule of Faith ... of every English Christian.'[5] Constitutionally, Thomas Rogers, their first expositor, was right to entitle the first edition of his book *The English Creede* (1585),[6] and Burnet was right when in the Preface to his own exposition of the Articles (1699) he described them as 'the sum of our doctrine, and the confession of our faith'.[7] So, too, the Royal Declaration of 1628, which is still prefixed to the Articles in the Prayer Book, in accordance with the 1662 Act of Uniformity, affirms that 'the Articles of the Church of England ... do contain the true Doctrine of the Church of England agreeable to God's Word'. To the question: what version of Christianity does the Church of England hold? and, more particularly, where does she stand with reference to the Reformation cleavages? the Thirty-nine

---

[5] Erik Routley, *Creeds and Confessions* (London: Duckworth, 1962), p. 112.
[6] Full title: *The English Creede; consenting with the True, Auncient Catholique and Apostolique Church in al the points and articles of Religion which everie Christian is to knowe and beleeve that would be saved* (Two parts: 1585, 1587.)
[7] Gilbert Burnet, *An Exposition of the Thirty-nine Articles of the Church of England*, ed. James R. Page (1839), p. vii

Articles still supply the only legally valid answer. They were compiled to be the domestic creed of *ecclesia Anglicana*, and such, officially, they remain.

3.2. The Development of Different Traditions of Interpretation

The Thirty-nine Articles are sometimes accused of ambiguity and equivocation, but the charge is both misguided and untrue. They are not in the least ambiguous in the answers which they give to the central theological questions of the conflict with Rome: the sense in which Scripture is the rule of faith (Articles 6, 8, 19, 20, 21); the state and need of fallen man (9, 10, 13); the nature, ground, and means of justification (11, with the Homily referred to: 'Of the Salvation of Mankind'); the meaning of grace (17); the assurance of faith (17); the identification of true churches and clergy (19, 23, 36); the nature, number, and operation of the sacraments (25-30); the Papal claim to supremacy (37); and the propriety of a national church putting its own house in order under the direction of the civil ruler (34, 37). Nor, again, are the Articles equivocal in their censures upon the beliefs and practices which had controlled medieval popular piety: the doctrine of purgatory (22), indulgences (22), image- and relic-worship (22), invocation of saints (22), works of supererogation (14), the immaculate conception (15), worship in an incomprehensible foreign language (24), transubstantiation (28), communion in one kind (30), the mass-sacrifice (31), and the belief that 'those five commonly called Sacraments' were rites of the same nature as baptism and the Lord's Supper (25). Nor are the Articles at all indefinite in their counter-statements to Anabaptist eccentricities: anti-Trinitarianism (1, 5); Arianism and docetism (2, 3, 4); the doctrine of the 'internal word' (6); a new Marcionism, denying the Unity of the two Testaments (7); antinomianism (7); Pelagianism (9-12); perfectionism (15); Novatianism (16); fatalism (17); the belief that sincerity in any form of religion will save without faith in Christ (18); disregard for the church visible and its authority in matters of faith and order (19, 20, 23, 33, 34); depreciation of the sacraments as means of grace (25, 27, 28) ; Donatism (26); antipaedobaptism (27); denial of the authority of civil rulers over Christians (37), especially in connection with military service (37) and oath-taking (39); and a communistic denial of property-rights among Christians (38).[8]

As their title declares, the Articles were drawn up 'for the avoiding of diversities of opinions, and for the establishing of consent touching true religion,'[9] a purpose which deliberate ambiguity would actually have defeated; since ambiguity is a device not for avoiding diversities of opinions, but for allowing them. In fact, however, in relation to the disputes that they were meant to settle they are, as Routley says, 'singularly precise'.[10] Moreover, their determinations of these disputes are such as to line them up at every point with the rest of the confessions of Reformed (Calvinistic) Christendom. In expounding the Articles, Thomas Rogers demonstrated at every point their substantial concord with their continental counterparts and when in 1581 *A Harmony of the Confessions of Faith of the Orthodox and Reformed Churches* was published at Geneva, the Thirty-nine Articles had a place in it.

It is not true, then, that the Articles are ambiguous. But what is true is that they are studiedly minimal in their requirements, and conscientiously leave many secondary questions open. As Pearson wrote in 1660 :

> The book [of Articles] ... is not, nor is pretended to be, a complete body of divinity ... but an enumeration of some truths, which upon and since the Reformation have been denied by some persons; who upon denial are thought unfit to have any cure of

---

[8] For information about the Anabaptist views that the Articles controverted, cf Hooper's letter to Bullinger on June 25, 1549, and that of Micronius to Bullinger on August 14, 1551 (*Original Letters*, [P.S., 1851] I. 65f. , II. 574). Cf G. H. Williams, *The Radical Reformation* (London: Weidenfeld and Nicolson, 1962), pp. 778ff.

[9] This follows the title of the Forty-two, which declared them to have been agreed on 'for the avoiding of controversy in opinions, and the establishment of a godly concord in certain matters of religion.'

[10] Routley, *Creeds and Confessions* p. 99. The best source of information about the theological intentions of each Article is still the section of 'Notes and illustrations, appended to Hardwick's *History of the Articles* (2nd edition, 1859), which all later expositors follow.

souls in this Church or realm...'[11]

They lay down as much as was thought necessary, in the mid-sixteenth-century situation, to secure catholic faith and ordered life in the reformed Church of England, but beyond that minimum they do not seek to go. This is the truth that lies behind Burnet's observation, often quoted and commonly misunderstood, that the Articles are at certain points 'conceived in large and general words', the 'literal and grammatical sense' of which admits of more than one explanation.[12] This only means that at certain points the Articles decline to decide against any of the possible alternatives. Though sharp-edged against the intolerable-seeming errors of Rome and the Anabaptists,[13] and full and exact on all the central issues of the gospel, the Articles are nowhere narrower or more exclusive than they have to be, and their definitions were, it seems, always made as broad and comprehensive as was thought consistent with theological safety.

---

[11] J .Pearson, *Minor Theological Works*. ed. W. Churton (1844), II.215.

[12] Gilbert Burnet, *Exposition* p. 11. Burnet gives as an example Article 3, on Christ's descent into hell, where the deleting in 1563 of an allusion to 1 Peter 3:18 left three possible interpretations open.

[13] In 1563, four of the Forty-two Articles that were clearly aimed against Anabaptist views (10, 39, 41, 42, against fatalism, denial of the resurrection of the body, millennarianism, and universalism, respectively) were dropped; presumably because (i) the points at issue were already safeguarded elsewhere (on fatalism, cf the present Article 17; on denial of the resurrection, which the Creeds affirm, cf 17, 18; on the licentiousness and anarchy to which millennial hopes gave rise, cf 7, 37); (ii) Anabaptist influence had so waned that these censures were no longer needed. But at the same time the anti-Romanism of the code was made more pronounced, the additions and alterations being in several cases a direct counter to decisions made by the Council of Trent (1545-1563): eg denial of canonical status to the Apocrypha (6); additions against transubstantiation (a phrase in 28 and 29); repudiation of the doctrine of seven sacraments (25), and of communion in one kind (30); strengthened statements on clerical marriage, services in the vernacular, and the mass (32, 24, 31); and substitution of 'the Romish doctrine' for 'the doctrine of school authors' in 22, to show that it was Tridentine teaching that was being condemned. For a conspectus of the alterations made in the 1563 revision, see Edgar C. S. Gibson, *The Thirty-nine Articles*, (London: Methuen, 1898), pp. 32ff.

As a statement of faith, then, the Articles are conscientiously minimal. Also, they are consciously eclectic. They set out the Trinitarian faith of the ecumenical creeds (1-5) as biblical and necessary to salvation (6-8), together with Augustine's doctrine of sin (9-10); Lutheran teaching on justification, grace, and the church (11-21, 23, 34, 37), as given in the Augsburg Confession of 1530 and the Wurtemberg Confession of 1552 (used in the 1563 revision); and sacramental teaching of the Swiss sort (25-29), with at one point an anti-Lutheran edge (29). So far as they bear the impress of a single mind, it is Cranmer's (Parker, chief architect of the 1563 revision, was Cranmer's devoted disciple), and Cranmer was an eclectic theologian whose forte was not innovation, but discrimination. Moreover, during the century and a half between the making of the Articles and the appearance of Burnet's exposition of them, the pendulum of Anglican theological opinion was swinging all the time: from the modified Lutheran outlook of Cranmer and his colleagues to the more scholastic Calvinist position of Jewel, Whitgift, Perkins, and Whitaker; thence, partly in reaction, partly through Greek patristic and philosophical influence, to the 'churchy' Arminianism of the Carolines and the moralistic Arminianism of the Latitudinarians, men like Chillingworth, the Cambridge Platonists, and Burnet himself. All this being so, it is no wonder that different interpretative traditions grew up, different theologians expounding the Articles from different basic stand-points and in the light of different estimates of the significance of the Reformation.

Expositions have been broadly of three types, which we may call 'Reformed', 'Latitudinarian' and 'Catholic'. Authors in the first group, regarding both the questions and the answers of Reformation theology as perennially the right ones, which the Bible calls theologians in every age to make their own, prize the Articles as a kerygmatic document of lasting importance. Authors in the second group, viewing the Reformation chiefly as a release from medieval superstition, value the Articles mainly as a classical protest against such superstition, in the name of history and common sense.

Authors in the third group, looking to the first five

Christian centuries for 'catholic' standards of faith and life, generally care little for the positive emphases of the Reformation, but see it as a needed reaction against un-catholic accretions, and view the Articles as having effected a real, if incomplete and even at some points unintended, restoration of primitive catholicity.

The main expositors of the first type were Thomas Rogers, *The English Creede* (the revised edition of 1607, re-titled *The Catholic Doctrine Believed and Professed in the Church of England*, was reprinted by the Parker Society in 1854); T. P. Boultbee, *A Commentary on the Thirty-nine Articles forming an Introduction to the Theology of the Church of England* (5th edition, 1880); and W. H. Griffith Thomas, *The Principles of Theology* (1930). (See too E. A. Litton, *Introduction to Dogmatic Theology* [1882-1892]; H. C. G. Moule, *Outlines of Christian Doctrine* [1889]).

The main work of the second type was and is Burnet's *Exposition* (1699), which remained a standard work for a century and a half (it was reissued with additional notes for students by James R. Page in 1839).

Works of the third class vary according to how far the writers lean towards Tridentine dogma on the one hand or Latitudinarian 'rationality' on the other. The main 'Catholic' stream of exposition, somewhat sacramentalist but not at all sacerdotalist, and as stoutly anti-Tridentine as anti-Calvinist, may be traced through the commentaries on the Articles by Bishop William Beveridge (1710), Bishop Harold Browne (1850), and Bishop E. C. S. Gibson (1897). Bishop A. P. Forbes' *Explanation of the Thirty-nine Articles* (1867-68) follows the Trent-ward lead of Newman's Tract 90 (1841) and the earlier attempt to reconcile the Anglican Articles with the Council of Trent by Franciscus à Sancta Clara (Christopher Davenport), *Paraphrastica Expositio Articulorum Confessionis Anglicanae* (1646: translated by F. G. Lee, 1865); while the 'liberal catholic' approach of E. J. Bicknell's *Theological Introduction to the Thirty-nine Articles* (1919; revised by H. J. Carpenter, 1955) is often reminiscent of Burnet.

Broadly speaking, the main cleavages between the three

schools of thought, at any rate during the past century of discussion, have been these:

(i) The first and second, against the third, deny that the Church of England needs anything more than the Articles specify to vindicate its catholic and apostolic character (no higher doctrine of the ministry, for instance, is needed).

(ii) The second and third, against the first, expound justification by faith legalistically rather than Christologically, treating faith as in some sense a meritorious work.

(iii) The third maintains, against the first and second, that the withdrawal in 1563 of the attacks which Articles 26 and 29 of the Forty-two had made on the *ex opere operato* view of the efficacy of the sacraments, and the real presence, implied a positive sanctioning of these views; also, that the present Article 31 is not directed against Tridentine teaching on the mass.

(iv) The first maintains, against the second and third, that Article 17 teaches the absolute freedom and sovereignty of divine grace in salvation, and that Article 19 implies that the invisible-visible distinction of Reformation theology is basic for a sound doctrine of the church.

(v) The second maintains, against the first and third, that in any case the theological concepts and convictions of biblical, patristic, and Reformation theology are not necessarily normative at every point for us today.

These cleavages will continue at least as long as both Bicknell and Griffith Thomas are read in theological colleges or vicarages, and meanwhile none of these three schools of thought can easily be denied the right to exist in the reformed Church of England, whatever our convictions may be about the issues that divide them. It is small wonder that, in face of this constantly shifting three-party debate, some moderns should conclude that the Anglican theological vocation is 'dialectical' rather than 'confessional', and that it is not the nature of Anglicanism to have a distinctive theology of its own, while others argue that these three traditions will yet grow into an ultimate synthesis, but that meanwhile none of them is more than relatively and provisionally valid. Were either line of thought correct, it would seem to follow that Anglican churches today are called to be latitudinarian in practice and doctrinally lax as a matter of theological principle; they should hold the ring, as it were, for the various combatants, but do nothing to hinder anyone's freedom of theological experiment at any point. We have met this idea already, and seen reason to reject it. If we accepted it, Anglican disunity on matters of faith would cease to be cause for distress; we should look on it as unity in the making, just as some already look on evil and sin as good in the making. But if we reject it, we have to face the fact that our disunity is a scandal, in the full biblical sense of that word – namely, a stumbling-block which threatens spiritual disaster – and one which only a renewing of the kind of faith into which the Articles seek to guide us will remove.

One further point belongs here. It is surely plain that the Articles, being over four centuries old, must be interpreted historically – "contextualized", to use the in-word – and taken to mean what they meant when first composed. Sometimes, however, in the heat of hostility to the Articles this gets forgotten, and in the intervals between assaults on the Articles for not speaking to modern questions at all critics attack them for speaking to modern questions in an unacceptable way. (Heads I win, tails you lose). Thus, a Jewish Christian attacked Article 13 ('Works done before the grace of Christ ... are not pleasing to God, forasmuch as they spring not of faith in Jesus Christ ... they have the nature of sin'), and also Article 18 ('They ... are to be had accursed that ... say, That every man shall be saved by the Law or Sect which he professeth'), because he saw these statements as slighting his non-Christian father, who was an admirer and follower of Jesus' teaching about God and about neighbour-love. But these Articles only echo Philippians 3:4-11 and Acts 4:12 respectively, and their wording addresses Reformation debates on good works and the universal need of Christ, and to censure them for not saying what he would say when speaking of his father is absurd. *Subscription and Assent* did well to stress the need for historical interpretation, and the relevant sentences from section 11 of the report may well be quoted here.[14]

> The Articles ought to be read in the light of the situation out of which they came, and to which they were addressed, and ... their words must be taken in the context and the sense they bore at the time of writing, and their statements construed in the light of the known views, assumptions and intentions of their authors. The accuracy with which it was possible to do this, and the awareness of the complexity of the issues involved, have, of course, varied considerably over the centuries. In the eighteenth century, for instance, the principle was appealed to explicitly by Daniel Waterland, who in *The Case of Arian Subscription* (1721), arguing against the right of Arians and Deists to give an altogether minimal assent to the Articles, condemned the view that 'these Articles may conscientiously be subscribed in any sense in which [men] themselves, by their own interpretation, could reconcile them to Scripture, without regard to the meaning and intention of the persons who first compiled or now imposed them'. The nineteenth century saw the most famous controversy of all connected with the question of subscription, that of Tract 90. It would be incorrect to say that Newman had abandoned the historical principle altogether. A fairer statement would be that he was applying the same principle to the answering of a new question, namely how much of common ground the Articles retained with Roman Catholicism, instead of the then customary one, how far they dissociated the Church of England from it. Owing to the limitations of the scholarship of his time regarding the issues and terminology of Reformation debate, he thought the Articles were more ambiguous than they actually were, and failed to see that the 'real and catholic sense' which he read into them was at many points inconsistent with the sense which an historically better informed interpreter would read out of them...

That is wisdom. No one complains that 'being of one substance with the Father' (the *homoousion* of the Nicene Creed) is a foolish or obscure phrase, or one we ought now to drop inasmuch as in modern culture 'substance' has for most people no metaphysical but only a chemical meaning. We know how to contextualize the

---

[14] *Subscription and Assent* pp. 13f.

homoousion in terms of fourth-century debate, and we do so routinely, and anyone who complains that the creed makes no clear sense here gets taken aside and told what it means by reference to what it meant originally. But if it is not a defect of the Nicene Creed to need contextualizing in fourth-century terms, it cannot fairly be seen as a defect of the Articles that they need contextualizing in sixteenth-century terms. Any interpreting and applying of the Articles without reference to the sixteenth-century situation will be suspect.

3.3. The Devaluing of Clerical Subscription

Just over a century ago, Hardwick stated the meaning of subscription to the Articles as follows:[15]

> Subscription to the Articles has been exacted with the hope of securing uniformity of doctrine in those Churchmen who deliberately assume the office of public teachers. It accordingly involves their own appropriation of the Articles as the exponent of their individual opinions – so far at least as such opinions bear on subjects which have been determined by authority in that code of doctrine; and, while pledging every clergyman to full and positive faith, subscription is the act by which he also formally renounces errors and corruptions which are there repudiated or proscribed. It does not indeed imply that every single definition in the Articles is capable of the same kind of proof, or that they are all in the same way needful to salvation ... yet even with respect to minor statements, some of which may be regarded as no more than probable opinions, and others as but matters of history and morals, every candidate for holy orders certifies his willingness to shape his future teaching by the public standard, and to yield unwavering assent to the propriety of all the code.

Since Hardwick wrote, however, a much lower and looser view of

---

[15] Charles Hardwick, *History of the Articles* (3rd edition, edited by F. Procter), pp. 219f.

the meaning of subscription has become current. There are at least three reasons for this.

3.3.1. First, the form of subscription has been altered.

Canon 36 of 1604, as we saw above, required subscription *ex animo* to the Articles (along with the Royal Supremacy and the Prayer Book) 'and to all things that are contained in them', as being 'agreeable to the Word of God'. This requirement remained when the Church was restored in 1662. Burnet thought clerical subscription 'a great imposition', and wished to end it altogether;[16] so did many Arian and Socinian clergy in the eighteenth century, in company with some Latitudinarians of a more respectable type, like Paley, who backed Blackburne's abortive 'Feathers Tavern Petition' for this purpose. Neither then nor since, however, did more than a minority want subscription abolished. But in 1865, as unanimously recommended by a Royal Commission (on which the evangelical spokesman was Henry Venn of the Church Missionary Society), the form of subscription was changed from 'I ... do willingly and from my heart subscribe to the Thirty-nine Articles ... and to all things therein contained' to a composite assent to Articles, Prayer Book, and Ordinal together – 'I believe the doctrine of the Church of England as therein contained [sc in all three] to be agreeable to the Word of God...'

That the substitution of a comprehensive for a particular assent was meant to render subscription less stringent is evident and certain. Yet as *Subscription and Assent* pointed out,[17]

> Contrary to what is sometimes supposed, the alteration in the form of subscription in 1865 did not in any way imply that henceforth a 'general' assent, in the sense of an incomplete assent, to the Articles would be legally adequate. In law, assent must be taken to mean 'complete legal acceptance'. This has

---

[16] Gilbert Burnet, *History of his Own Times* (1734), II. 634; cf *Exposition*, p. 7. Burnet had been instrumental in getting clerical subscription abolished at Geneva: *History*...II. 692f.

[17] *Subscription and Assent* section 8, p. 12.

been variously interpreted. A minimal view, associated with the names of Laud, Bramhall, and Ussher, maintained that the Articles were only 'Articles of peace' and that complete legal acceptance implies no more than an undertaking not to contradict them in public. At the other extreme, there have been those who believed that complete legal acceptance of the Articles implies inward commitment to their every proposition ... The Act of 1865 retained the word 'assent', and it is this, rather than any intentions expressed by individuals in the debates, which has legal force. Thus in law the situation remained essentially what it was.

Since then, the form of subscription has been changed once more. The new Canon C 15, 'Of the Declaration of Assent', opens thus:

1(1) The Declaration of Assent to be made under this Canon shall be in the form set out below:

PREFACE

The Church of England is part of the One, Holy, Catholic and Apostolic Church worshipping the one true God, Father, Son and Holy Spirit. She professes the faith uniquely revealed in the Holy Scriptures and set forth in the catholic creeds, which faith the Church is called upon to proclaim afresh in each generation. Led by the Holy Spirit, she has borne witness to Christian truth in her historic formularies, the Thirty-nine Articles of Religion, the Book of Common Prayer and the Ordering of Bishops, Priests and Deacons. In the declaration you are about to make will you affirm your loyalty to this inheritance of faith as your inspiration and guidance under God in bringing the grace and truth of Christ to this generation and making Him known to those in your care?

DECLARATION OF ASSENT

I, AB, do so affirm, and accordingly declare my belief in the faith which is revealed in the Holy Scriptures and set forth in the catholic creeds and to which the historic formularies of the Church of England bear witness; and in public prayer and administration of the sacraments, I will use only the forms of service which are authorised or allowed by Canon.

Naturally, since this form of words is meant to have moral as well as legal authority for all schools of Anglicans (which excludes any idea of pressuring one group in the interests of another), it is not written as Protestant evangelicals legislating for Protestant evangelicals might have written it. (It follows out, in fact, a suggestion made in *Subscription and Assent*.) What it says, however, is quite specific, and clearly expresses the following points, in which evangelicals have historically had a special interest:

(i)   The place of Holy Scripture as the primary source and standard of faith for God's church.

The subscriber professes 'belief in the faith which is *revealed in the Holy Scriptures*'. The statement in the Preface that that faith, the faith of the worldwide church, is *'uniquely* revealed in the Holy Scriptures' declares that as a source for knowledge of the faith Scripture is in a class by itself. Since the subscriber acknowledges 'the historic formularies of the Church of England' as bearing witness to that faith, he must be understood to be assenting to the principle of the sufficiency of Scripture as our ultimate source and final standard of belief; for that principle is stated clearly and in detail in Articles 6-8, 20, 21.

(ii)   The place of the Articles as a secondary standard of faith for Anglicans.

The Articles, along with the 1662 Prayer Book and Ordinal, are described in the Preface as the 'witness to Christian truth' which the Church of England has been 'led by the Holy Spirit' to bear. The linking of the three formularies is a reminder that authority attaches to the expression of faith in worship and ministry, as well as to the confession of it in creedal statements – although, of the three formularies only the Articles purport to define beliefs, and therefore only they can be appealed to as doing so. Acceptance of this estimate of the formularies as the Church of England's Spirit-led witness to God's truth gives them, on the one hand, a recognized positive status as guides, and on the other hand, a negative voice in evaluation. To the extent to which Anglican theologians, whether intentionally or not, go against the terms or purposes of the formularies, they must be held to have failed to further the Anglican witness to Christian truth, and their work will thus have only the force of a cautionary tale in the Anglican 'inheritance of faith'.

(iii) The authority of the Articles for the directing of ministry in the Church of England.

The subscriber affirms 'loyalty' to the Anglican 'inheritance of faith', as defined in the Preface, and accepts it to be his 'inspiration and guidance under God' for making known 'the grace and truth of Christ' to those to whom he ministers. 'Inspiration' in this context is a weighty word, signifying the means of understanding, insight and vision. 'Guidance' indicates an acknowledgement of the Articles' real authority, and readiness to follow where they lead. 'Under God' implies that, though the authority of these human formulations cannot be final, there is no appeal away from them save to the written Word of God, the given revelation itself. The following words, 'in bringing the grace and truth of Christ to this generation and making him known to those in your care,' give liberty, in face of present-day questions, to raise issues which the Articles do not raise and to develop one's thinking beyond the point where the formularies stop. But they give no liberty to disregard, denigrate, or contradict what the Articles actually teach. The profession of 'loyalty to this inheritance of faith' should imply, rather, that one accepts the theology of the formularies as one's starting-point and intends that this should show in one's ministry.

Such is the present state of play with regard to the form of assent. We turn now to some further aspects of the subscription story, aspects which are much less encouraging and present some ominous problems.

3.3.2. Second, excessive latitude of interpretation has been claimed by subscribers.

Arguing that only a strictly historical interpretation, in terms of the compilers' meaning as evidenced by their words, was legitimate, Hardwick went on to declare:[18]

> The method of interpreting particular Articles was made a further subject of discussion from the time of their first appearance; one claiming to subscribe them with the mental reservation – 'so far as in my judgement they agree with Holy Scripture' [a reference to Puritan recalcitrants under Elizabeth] ; a second, questioning the absolute obligation of the test, or struggling to evade it whenever it appeared to vary from the language of an older school or system of theology [a side-kick, apparently, at subscription of the type advocated in Newman's *Tract 90*] but reluctant though we be to stigmatize subscribers of this kind as utterly disloyal to the Church ... such an exercise of 'private judgement' is assuredly incompatible with unity, and adverse to the health of all religious associations.

During the past century, however, habits of mental reservation and taking Articles in non-natural private senses became almost the rule in some quarters, and the melancholy truth of Hardwick's closing observation has been illustrated time and again.

3.3.3. Third, the significance of the act of subscription has been minimized.

As early as the seventeenth century, Bramhall and others were urging that the Articles were not strictly a confession so much as 'articles of peace, 'which Anglicans, clerical and lay, were not obliged to believe, but only to refrain from openly contradicting. (Burnet, to his credit, rejected this view.) The idea that the act of subscribing need not of itself imply full assent has in recent years been taken up again, and fairly run to death. Bishops, over-anxious not to bind burdens on sensitive consciences, have eviscerated the ordinand's declaration of assent by expounding it to him in terms of negations. The late Archbishop Garbett wrote,

> I myself explain to my ordinands that their subscription is an

---

[18] Hardwick, *History of the Articles* p. 220f.

expression of loyalty to the faith of the Church, and that no man could honestly subscribe if he rejected belief in the supernatural, or held that either the Romans or the Puritans were right in their controversies with our Church.[19]

The late Bishop Rawlinson wrote,

> In practice, the assent to the Articles is now understood to commit the clergy only to a generally Anglican theology, neither Roman Catholic on the one hand nor exclusively 'Protestant' on the other.[20]

What Dr Garbett meant by 'the faith of the Church' and Dr Rawlinson by 'a generally Anglican theology' can only be surmised, but plainly what they had in mind was something less than actually believing all the Articles and going on from there. Their statements appear to be framed as an answer to the question: how little need a man's subscription mean? Perhaps this was the only question about subscription that they were ever asked; certainly, this is the only question about subscription that Anglicans generally have asked for the past hundred years. But the right question to ask is: how *much* should the act of subscription mean? Is it not high time that Anglicans faced this question afresh?

It would doubtless be very foolish to become starry-eyed at this point. As no changes in the form of subscription will restore the true significance of the act of subscribing as long as folk ask only how little the act need mean, and how little one need feel bound by it, so, humanly speaking, it is unlikely that subscribers' basic attitudes will quickly change. When coinage has been devalued it is hard to revalue it upward (think of the British pound over the past thirty years!), and now that subscription has been devalued for more than a century, re-establishing in Anglican minds how much it ought to mean, and thus re-sensitizing

---

[19] C. Garbett, *The Claims of the Church of England* (London: Hodder and Stoughton, 1947), p.35.
[20] A. E. J. Rawlinson, *The Anglican Communion in Christendom* (London: SPCK, 1960), p. 7.

consciences about it, will be a long and arduous task. It is always easier to pull something down than to build it up again, and to continue what has become customary than to change it. There are clergy who luxuriate in the loose and lawless pluralism of thought for which the Church of England seems currently to have settled, and when the propriety of this pluralism is challenged they may be expected to fight back. But I wish to challenge it all the same, and shall therefore return to the question of how much subscription ought to mean before my argument finishes; for surely it is plain from what has been said that some rethinking is needed here, however hard it may be to engage my fellow-Anglicans in this task.

4. A PLACE FOR THE ARTICLES

The Thirty-nine Articles are framed so directly in terms of sixteenth-century controversy in England that the provinces of the Anglican communion that began to emerge overseas nearly three centuries later could hardly have been expected to take them over as their own confession of faith.

Nor in fact have they done so in any practical way. It is often observed that the nineteenth resolution of the Lambeth Conference of 1888 declared explicitly that new Anglican provinces need not 'be bound to accept in their entirety the Thirty-nine Articles' – though it is not always noticed that, as I pointed out earlier, the resolution goes on to state that, as a condition of full communion with existing Anglican bodies, new provinces must give 'satisfactory evidence that they hold substantially the same doctrine as our own, and that *their clergy subscribe Articles in accordance with the express statements of our own standards of doctrine and worship.*' But this resolution as we also saw, seems to have been honoured more in the breach than in the observance; for it is observable that the Articles have no place in current accounts of Anglican unity. The 1930 Lambeth Conference, for instance, in a statement often treated as definitive, affirmed that the churches of the Anglican communion are a company

> whose faith has been grounded in the doctrines ... for which the Church of England has always stood;

but these are then described thus :

> the Catholic faith in its entirety: that is to say, the truth of Christ, contained in Holy Scripture; stated in the Apostles' and Nicene Creeds; expressed in the Sacraments of the Gospel and the rites of the Primitive Church as set forth in the Book of Common Prayer with its various local adaptations; and safeguarded by the

historic threefold Order of the Ministry.[1]

There is no reference here to the Articles at all.

One effect, therefore, on the Church of England of being part of the Anglican communion is that pressure to leave the Articles in a theological lumber-room, as having no further significant part to play in shaping the faith and life of English Christians, is constant and strong. If daughter churches have done it (not denounced or denied the Articles, but simply dismissed them as of merely historical interest, and remote interest at that), should not the mother church do the same? What this course would mean practically is that no questions about the present-day relevance of the Articles would be asked; no appeal to the Articles as a standard would be made; no dialogue between the Articles and ourselves would be entered into; no estimate of their quality as a confession would be attempted. The Articles would retain their legal and constitutional position and be duly subscribed, but they would have no moral authority or theological impact in Anglican intellectual life. But, you will say, that is just about the way things are at present! Exactly; and there is no lack of voices to assure us that it is better so, and nothing else would ever make sense. The Articles, we are told, do not represent the general mind of the Church in these days; in the post-Enlightenment evolution, or revolution, of religious thought all save a few freaks and shellbacks have moved on, in Monty Python manner, to something completely different; therefore let sleeping Articles lie, for they do not speak to our condition. However, in this essay I am arguing that by biblical and theological as well as constitutional and historical right the Articles ought to count for far more in Anglican theologizing, and in the education of clergy and laity, than they currently do, and I challenge the assumption that the best way for the Church of England to go in its use or non-use of the Articles is the way that much of the Anglican communion has understandably if unfortunately gone.

---

[1] *The Lambeth Conferences, 1867-1930*, p. 246.

I shall argue my case in two stages. In this chapter I shall offer answers to three questions: (1) What authority may the Articles claim? (2) What functions can the Articles fulfil? (3) What response do the Articles require? In the final chapter I shall tackle a fourth question: How should we use the Articles in Church life?

4.1. What Authority may the Articles Claim ?

My answer to this question is: the authority proper to a creed.

To describe the Articles, as I do in this essay, as a creed – the domestic creed of the Church of England – may at first sight appear merely naive, for it is the custom nowadays to keep the word 'creed' for the ecumenical creeds (the Apostles' and Nicene, with or without the Athanasian, which was never formally accepted in the East and, indeed, is not strictly speaking a creed at all), and to contrast these creeds with the Reformation confessions as if they were two entirely different sorts of thing. The creeds (it is said) were in origin pastoral documents, versions of the Trinitarian baptismal profession which were gradually enlarged into catechetical texts, and as such became gestures of unity by which the undivided church testified against mortal misbelief; whereas the confessions were occasional and polemical statements, produced *ad hoc* by particular theologians as manifestos of dissent within Christendom, and having authority only in the particular Christian body from which each came. The creeds are primary statements of faith; the confessions are secondary, presupposing the creeds and standing as a postscript to them. Creeds can be used liturgically, but not confessions. The creeds and the confessions differ in form, the creeds being short, organic, and positive, whereas the confessions are elaborate, subdivided, and controversial. Also, they differ in substance, the creeds centring upon the Triune Godhead in creation and redemption, whereas the confessions focus on anthropology, soteriology, and even church order and politics. Again, they differ in character, for the creeds emerged as a body of truth to form and express the faith of learners, whereas the confessions were drawn up to test the orthodoxy of teachers. From these and other related contrasts, the conclusion is often drawn that, whereas the ecumenical creeds are integral and necessary to the church's life in every age, the Reformation confessions – the Articles among them – are products of a bygone day which have served their turn and can now, in this ecumenical era, be dispensed with.

But the conclusion does not follow, for the contrast between the creeds and the confessions is not as deep or far-reaching as is supposed. The differences noted above, though real, are superficial and external only; they reflect merely the different historical circumstances and controversial concerns by which the creeds and the confessions respectively were called forth. Theologically, and in terms of themselves, both have the same nature. For the creeds are confessions of Christ against views that in some way deny Him, just as the Reformation statements are; and the Reformation statements are standards of evangelical orthodoxy, just as the ecumenical creeds are. Both exist to safeguard and express the unity and purity of Christian faith against the depredations of heresy. Both were formally received in the church as means of discharging the church's responsibility to proclaim and preserve the gospel. The basic relation between the creeds and the confessions is not one of contrast, but of continuity and development: the confessions supplement the creeds by drawing out the soteriology which they imply, just as the Athanasian Creed supplemented the Nicene, and the Nicene the Apostles', by amplified statements on the Trinity and the incarnation. In the words of W. H. Griffith Thomas:

> As we follow in order the three Creeds themselves, the Apostles', the Nicene, and the Athanasian, we find that there is a tendency to elaboration, to a fuller theological statement, and to an explanation of what is involved in the original summary of belief. The confessions of faith in the sixteenth century are really only an extension, prolongation, and development of the same process.[2]

---

[2] Griffith Thomas, *Principles of Theology*, p. xxv.

This has been cogently shown by Gustaf Aulen in his book, *Reformation and Catholicity* (Eng. tr. 1962). Taking 'confession' as his basic idea, Aulen demonstrates that the patristic confession (the creeds) and the Reformation confession (the confessional statements of the various national churches) are 'defensive confessions' clarifying and fencing 'the biblical, apostolic confession'.[3] The content of each confession, Aulen argues, is substantially the same. The New Testament confession of Jesus as Lord (*Kyrios*) and Christ had four focal points: the fact that the man Jesus lives, the risen Master; the fact that He died for sins upon the cross; the fact that He will come again, for the final salvation of His people; and the fact that He is God the Son, co-creator with His Father. The patristic confession, organized round the thought of Jesus as God incarnate and so as divine Saviour, was centred on the same four points, guarding them against docetism (the Apostles' Creed) and Arianism (the Nicene Creed). The Reformation confession of Jesus as the One in and through whom sinners are justified by faith alone and saved by sovereign grace was an elucidation and defence of the same apostolic confession, this time against a semi-Pelagian doctrine of salvation by meritorious churchmanship. In substance and purpose, Aulen maintains, the three confessions are one. All that differs is the relative emphasis and degree of elaboration at various points. Of the Reformation confession he writes:[4]

> It is, of course, true that the Reformation confession does not enjoy such universal recognition as the confession of the ancient church. It is the confession of only a part of Christendom ... It may seem presumptuous, therefore, to try to designate it as one of the principal Christian confessions. Nevertheless if we dare claim this distinction for it, we can do so only on the basis that it stands in positive agreement with the confession of the ancient church and especially with that of the New Testament.

---

[3] Gustaf Aulen, *Reformation and Catholicity* (Edinburgh: Oliver and Boyd, 1962), p. 91.
[4] Ibid., p. 121.

That the Thirty-nine Articles claim 'positive agreement with the confession of the ancient church' is clear from the fact that they begin by recapitulating the witness of the creeds to the Godhead and incarnation (1-5), and approving the creeds as biblical (8); thus they show that their purpose is to cleave to the faith of the creeds, and to preclude any lapses from it. That they claim 'positive agreement with the confession of ... the New Testament' is too obvious to need proof. They claim, in other words, to be what the ecumenical creeds are, explanatory echoes of the apostolic witness to Christ, and to exercise the same kind of authority as the creeds do. And any responsible assessment of the Articles must begin by taking this claim seriously.

The grounds on which it is sometimes maintained that the Articles have not the nature of a creedal statement are quite unsubstantial. To the argument that they are not a creed because they are not a complete body of divinity, it is enough to reply that, complete or not, they contain a great deal more than the ecumenical creeds themselves do. To the argument that they are not a creed because they include statements on Anglican domestic order and discipline, one need only say that this means they are more than a creed – not less! The argument that they are not a creed because they were brought out partly with a political motive, to settle strife and enable men to live together, is answered by the consideration that exactly the same was true of the Nicene Creed. The argument that they are not a creed because they have never given rise to an Anglican 'confessional' theology like the Lutheran is sufficiently met by pointing out that there has never been such a confessionalism in the Reformed churches either, yet Reformed theology is as clear as Lutheran about the identical nature of patristic creeds and sixteenth-century confessions.[5] The fact remains that the Thirty-nine Articles exhibit not only the same doctrine as other Reformation confessions do, but also the same

---

[5] See Karl Barth, *Church Dogmatics*, 1.2. (Edinburgh: T. and T. Clark, 1956), pp. 620-60, a classic discussion of the nature and significance of the confessional process.

concern to identify the faith they confess with the faith of the Fathers and the New Testament, and the same conviction that the road which they fence is, in fact, the highroad of catholicity, from which Romans and Anabaptists alike had gone astray. Like the rest of the Reformation confessions, the Articles are a domestic creed, and their authority must be understood accordingly.

What, now, is the authority to which a creed, ecumenical or domestic, may justly lay claim? Articles 8, 20, and 21 effectively define this for us. The authority of ecclesiastical statements of faith is not the inherent authority of pronouncements issuing from an infallible source, as Rome wrongly supposes, but the derived authority of a faithful echo, exposition, and application of 'God's Word written' (20) in its witness to God's living and personal Word, His own Son.

Creedal and confessional statements emerge at times of crisis in church life, when it seems that, unless the apostolic faith is clarified afresh, error will simply overwhelm it. At such times, the evangelical conscience reacts by publicly reaffirming the biblical faith as clearly as possible, in direct antithesis to the various falsehoods that threaten it. Such reaffirmations are always made in the name of the church universal, in the sense that they enshrine the strong conviction that any and every Christian, faced with this situation, would be under obligation to speak out in these same terms. Thus, simply by being made, these confessional statements summon all who claim to be Christians to consider whether what they affirm is not right. And when a particular church writes creedal statements of this sort into its constitution, it perpetuates this summons to every generation of its sons. So, each of the three Creeds, and with them the Thirty-nine Articles as a whole, now in effect cry out to every generation of Anglicans: At such-and-such a time, in face of such-and-such aberrations, the church to which you belong committed itself to the following affirmations and denials, for the preserving of biblical truth and the defence and confirmation of the gospel: do you not agree that these affirmations and denials were rightly made? And will you not therefore undertake to maintain equivalent affirmations and denials in your own situation?

This shows us what authority creeds and confessions may claim. They come to us as prior judgements, time-honoured judgements, on specific issues relating to the faith of Christ, as set forth in the Scriptures. They come to us as corporate decisions first made by the church centuries ago, and now confirmed and commended to us by the corroborative testimony of all later generations that have accepted them, down to our time. Thus, the Articles come to us backed by the approval of millions of Anglican worshippers over four centuries, and in particular of the hundreds of thousands of clergy who have subscribed them; while the three Creeds come to us with the backing of a far greater cloud of witnesses even than that. But, however great the number of those who, by accepting these formulations themselves, effectively commend them to us, infallibility is not at any point conferred upon them. The argument, sometimes heard, that the Creeds may safely be taken as a rule of faith because the whole world church has so long accepted them, whereas we cannot have similar confidence in the Articles because they have not been acknowledged by so great a number, does not go to the root of the matter. Even the Creeds remain human; we never dare treat them as intrinsically inerrant, no matter how many millions of people endorse them. The Creeds and the Articles alike come to us as venerable commentaries on, and primary expositions of, Holy Scripture; no more, and no less. Because they are no more than this, none of us is free from the responsibility of testing and measuring them by the Scriptures which they seek to expound before we finally accept them (as Article 8 says of the three Creeds, and as Article 20 says by implication of Article 8). But because they are no less than this, and because the church of which we are part has ventured to commit itself to them as sound expositions, none of us is free to neglect, or ignore, or slight them. It is a prime obligation for Anglicans to take full account of the expository formulations to which our church has bound itself; and to ignore them, as if we were certain that the Spirit of God had no hand in them, is no more warrantable than it is to treat them as divinely inspired and infallible.

We conclude, then, that the authority to which the Articles

may lay claim is the authority of *faithful witness*: the authority, that is, of a true echo and application of the biblical message. And the proper ground for endorsing them and, in the case of the clergy, consenting to subscribe them, is that one should have tested them by the Scriptures which they profess to expound and found them sure in their grasp of the Word of God.

4.2. *What Functions can the Articles Fulfil?*

We may well tune in to this question by reviewing the five uses which the world church has made of creedal statements, both ecumenical and domestic, down the centuries.

Use one is *declaratory*. In face of confusion, error and theological war these statements have been set up as banners, manifestos and rallying-points to show where folk stand and what they are not prepared to give up. Evangelical doctrinal bases have the same role. Thus to declare is, of course, to discriminate: it is to label some views true and others false, and to identify the former as the only acceptable basis for that kind and degree of togetherness which is being promoted and safeguarded. Thus to declare is also, however, to establish and proclaim oneness among those who accept the declaration. Declaration not only divides; it also unites.

Use two is *didactic*. These statements have been used in conjunction with Scripture to teach the faith.

Use three is *defensive* and *denunciatory*. Creedal statements have been used, still in conjunction with Scripture, as a yardstick for identifying heresy and a weapon for combating it.

Use four is *disciplinary*. Creedal statements have in many cases been given constitutional status, to function as limits to the beliefs of clergy and sometimes others too. Penalties have been imposed on those who transgress these limits.

Use five is *doxological*. The Apostles' and Nicene Creeds have been used in worship by Roman Catholics, Anglicans, Lutherans, Orthodox and, with less consistency, Presbyterians, as a celebration of God's mighty acts of creation and redemption corresponding to the recital of historical deliverances in the Psalms.

Which of these functions could the Articles fulfil today? Which do we need them to fulfil? Historically, they were intended to fulfil four main functions.

First, they were meant to act as the Church of England's theological identity-card, showing what she stood for in a split and warring Christendom. As such, the Articles were intended to be a title-deed to catholic status. Catholicity and apostolicity, to our Reformers, had nothing to do with an (unproveable) ministerial succession, but were matters entirely of doctrine. The third canon of 1604 claimed that the Church of England is 'a true apostolical church, teaching and maintaining the doctrine of the apostles.' The Articles were drawn up to make good this claim, (which, of course, antedates 1604; it goes back to the Reformers), and to show that the English Reformation, so far from being, as Rome supposed, a lapse from catholicity and apostolicity on the part of *ecclesia Anglicana,* was actually a recovery of these qualities through recovery of the authentic apostolic faith. Not for nothing did Rogers entitle the final edition of his exposition of the Articles 'The Catholic Doctrine of the Church of England'.

Second, the Articles were meant to safeguard the truth of the gospel, for the good of souls, the welfare of the church itself, and the glory of God. When Parker and fourteen other bishops wrote to Elizabeth in 1566 asking her to give the royal assent to a bill requiring subscription to the 1563 Articles, a bill which she had hitherto blocked (it was a first draft of the bill finally carried in 1571), the first three reasons which they gave for making this request were:[6]

> First, the matter itself toucheth the glory of God, the advancement of true religion, and the salvation of Christian souls, and therefore ought principally, chiefly, and before all

---

[6] *Correspondence of Archbishop Parker* (P.S., 1853), p. 293.

other things, to be sought. Secondly, in the book which is now desired to be confirmed, are contained the principal Articles of Christian religion most agreeable to God's word ... Thirdly, divers and sundry errors, and namely such as have been in this realm wickedly and obstinately by the adversaries of the Gospel defended, are by the same Articles condemned.

The Articles were intended to ensure that the gospel of justification by faith and salvation by grace, so long lost before the Reformation, should not be lost to the church again.

Third, as their title indicated, the Articles were meant to bring unity and order into the church ('the establishing of consent touching true religion'), and this in the realms of both doctrine and discipline. They were meant to guard the pulpit as the Prayer Book guarded the reading-desk, and so, in Henson's phrase, 'protect the people from heretical parsons.' They were meant also as doctrinal standards for interpreting the Prayer Book.

Parker's fourth reason for asking Elizabeth to demand subscription to the Articles was that:[7]

the approbation of the Articles by your Majesty shall be a very good mean to establish and confirm all your Highness' subjects in one consent and unity of true doctrine, to the great quiet and safety of your Majesty and this your realm; whereas now, for want of Articles of doctrine by law to be declared, great distraction and dissension of minds is at this present among your subjects.

The supposition that enforced uniformity of doctrine would produce spontaneous unanimity of judgement may seem naive to us today, yet there is no question that the Articles had a theologically stabilizing effect, both under Elizabeth and later.

Fourth, the Articles were meant to set bounds to the comprehensiveness of the Church of England. It was always intended that the reformed Church of England should be as

---

[7] Ibid., p. 294.

comprehensive as possible, and to that end the Articles were made as broad as possible, as we saw. But the comprehensiveness intended was an evangelical comprehensiveness: not what Dr. Vidler has called the 'unprincipled syncretism' of 'a sort of league of religions',[8] the state of affairs which would result if one should, as Bishop J. C. Ryle put it,

> declare the Church a kind of Noah's Ark, within which every kind of opinion and creed shall dwell safe and undisturbed, and the only terms of communion shall be willingness to come inside and let your neighbour alone,[9]

but the comprehensiveness that results from keeping doctrinal requirements down to the minimum and allowing the maximum of flexibility and variety on secondary matters. The Articles are in this sense minimal (they are the shortest of the Reformation confessions.) But they were meant to ensure that all Anglican clergy, whatever their views on other matters, should unite in teaching an Augustinian doctrine of sin and a Reformed doctrine of justification and grace – should, in other words, unite in proclaiming what the Reformers took to be the New Testament gospel.

Do these four jobs – identifying the Church of England in Christendom, preserving the apostolic 'word of faith', guarding the pulpit against anti-evangelical heresy, circumscribing comprehensiveness with the gospel – still need doing today? If we allow that the church is called of God to be 'the pillar and ground of the truth' (1 Timothy 3:15), and has corporately the responsibility which it assigns to its clergy individually, to 'banish and drive away all erroneous and strange doctrines contrary to God's Word,' and if we further allow that the Reformation decisions against Rome were essentially right, and did in fact mark the recovery of the apostolic gospel (which, it is hoped, few would dispute), then clearly we must say that these jobs do still need doing. But, we ask,

---

[8] Alec Vidler, *Essays in Liberality* (London: SCM, 1957), p. 166.
[9] J. C. Ryle, *Principles for Churchmen* (1884), p. xxiv.

are the Articles, in view of their age, still able to help to do them? To which the reply must be that they are, just as the Creeds are (and the Creeds are far older!). How can the Creeds and Articles help to perform these tasks today? By the questions which they put to us, and the admonitions with which they challenge us. Creeds and confessions, as we saw, are formally adopted by the church as reassertions of the gospel in face of particular errors. The very form of their counter to these errors reflects a particular view of what the gospel is. Whether or not the errors in question survive to future generations (in fact, most of those with which the Creeds and Articles deal do survive, but our present argument would stand even if they did not), the view of the gospel which these statements enshrine remains as a permanent challenge to all who come after. Thus, the Apostles' and Nicene Creeds challenge every generation of the world church: do you still stand with us on the Trinity? on the Incarnation? on the second coming of our Lord, and the Christian hope? If not, why not? Are not our positions scriptural? Go to the Bible and see. And if you find they are, will you not labour to teach and stress and defend these things in your day, as we did in ours? And the Articles, supplementing the Creeds, ask each generation of Anglicans further questions. Do you stand where we stand with regard to the sufficiency and supremacy of Scripture? the gravity of sin? justification by faith alone in and through Christ alone? the nature of the sacraments as seals of the gospel promise, means of grace because they are means to faith? loyalty to the gospel in word and sacrament as the sole decisive mark of the church? the dangerous, anti-evangelical tendency of Roman doctrines and practices? If these things are not at the centre of your faith and testimony, why not? Test these contentions by Scripture: is it not the case that where we are positive, the Bible was positive before us? And if we were right then to treat these points as evangelical essentials, ought not you to be seeking ways and means of proclaiming and vindicating them now?

It belongs to the Anglican theological vocation to live in continuous dialogue of this sort with the Creeds and the Articles. It is part of our proper theological discipline to expose ourselves to the questions which they ask us and to allow them constantly to challenge our lopsidedness, to correct our aberrations, to rebuke our 'negligences and ignorances,' to point us insistently back to the Scriptures, and to press upon us their classic clarifications of basic biblical and evangelical issues. Not that the dialogue should be one-sided: as the Articles cross-examine us in the name of Scripture, so we must cross-examine them with questions like: Why do you say this? what do you mean? what biblical warrant have you for it? (We must not, however, be surprised if we find, as others have found before us, that the Articles can give very satisfactory replies to such questions!) No Anglican has any business to try and evade this instructive and corrective dialogue, and anyone who has in any measure experienced the benefit of it will regard the man who does try to evade it as, not merely an inadequate Anglican, but foolish into the bargain. One test of the quality of a creed is the fruitfulness of this kind of dialogue with it. By this test, the Articles must be rated a very good creed indeed. In this way, then, they may still play a vital part in the theological life of twentieth-century Anglicanism, by ensuring that, while we address ourselves to new problems and preoccupations, we do not lose touch with the old gospel from which the answers to modern perplexities must be drawn. There is no greater service that they could do us.

4.3. *What Response do the Articles Require?*

If there is any substance in what we have been saying, it is clear that we may not just casually cast the Articles off because they are old. Until they are decisively refuted from Scripture (which has not been done yet), we have no warrant for rejecting them, or for relaxing the requirement of clerical subscription. Nor, as we saw earlier, have we any warrant for treating subscription as a traditional formality, having no existential significance for the subscriber save as a sign of loyalty to the Church of England as an institution. On the contrary, subscription to the Articles should indicate that a man has sought to test the Articles by Scripture and has found them 'agreeable to the Word of God'; that he approves, and desires to appropriate, their emphases, outlook, spirit, and the way of theological thinking which they embody; and that he is resolved to preach the gospel which they define, and to oppose all doctrines, however popular and fashionable, which explicitly or implicitly contravene them. The new form of subscription shows that the Church still wants its clergy to be men of this stamp, and for this one is thankful.

Some advocate re-wording or revising the Articles, but this plea is impracticable (for no re-wording could avoid changing the substance and thrust of what was being said, and no revision could command general agreement when it was done); further it is misconceived. You do not revise creeds; instead, you draw up further statements to supplement them. This is what Councils and Synods have historically done, and it was the right way for them to go. It was for this purpose that the Articles themselves were drawn up: they presupposed the Creeds, but went beyond them, dealing with issues which the Creeds did not directly handle. There is a case for a new Anglican statement today, presupposing both the Creeds and the Articles, and dealing on that basis with twentieth-century questions about (for instance) creation, providence, and common grace, on which the Articles scarcely touch. But it would be no more proper to alter the Articles than to alter the Creeds. Such action by a church could not be construed as other than a repudiation at some point of the old paths (which, inevitably, it really would be). None doubt that a church's catholicity would become suspect if she qualified her acceptance of the ecumenical Creeds. But if the historic claim that the Articles teach 'catholic doctrine' is sound, then any retreat from that doctrine will, to that extent, jeopardize the catholicity of Anglicanism.

The great need today is that Anglicans should face the Articles and enter into serious dialogue with them, and let them show us afresh (as they are well able to do) what the essentials of the gospel really are. Such a return to first principles is long overdue, and Anglican theology languishes for want of it. As Professor G. W. Bromiley has written:

> The current neglect or evasion or even defiance of the Articles is one of the greatest tragedies in modern Anglicanism. As they were conceived in the first instance, they gave hope of promoting both the unity in truth and the freedom under authority which are so necessary to the well-being of the Church. In spite of every

obstacle, they have not wholly failed of their purpose. But quite obviously they cannot today exercise their functions in the fruitful way which could mean so much not only for doctrinal but for spiritual and disciplinary health. No matter is more urgent than that glib misconceptions should be removed, the true historical purpose of the Articles appreciated, and the place restored to them in which positively and constructively, as well as negatively and critically, they can discharge their living and salutary function.[10]

Nothing better could be wished for the future of Anglicanism, and the well-being of Anglican churches, than that the Articles should regain among us the status which is theirs by theological right.

---

[10] *The Churchman* June 1959, p. 65.

5. A USE FOR THE ARTICLES

We turn now to practical matters. To what use can we put the Articles today? My answer can be stated in three words: assimilate, apply, augment.

5.1. Assimilation

It must by now be clear that I am an enthusiast for the Articles. They are more than a period piece, and merit an interest that is more than antiquarian. Coming from a time when the most basic question in Christianity, namely the terms of the gospel itself, was being fought out with scholarship and passion, they centre on fundamentals and define the gospel in a way that by biblical standards must be judged classic. They are thus abidingly relevant, and never more so than in a day like ours, when by reason of unsettlement resulting from what I think are unsound approaches to the Bible,[1] the churches of the Reformation have lost their certainty about this classic definition. For that is our current condition. Apart from the evangelical brotherhood (a minority), Protestant teachers at all levels have for some time now been relativizing the absolutes of the revealed gospel, apparently to make possible hopes of salvation for all the post- and non- and anti-Christian human community, and that has thrown lay-men into greater uncertainty about the content of the Christian message than has been known for centuries. This is as true of the Church of England as it is of any church, and hereby the apparently diminished importance is really enhanced; just as the lifeguard's importance is really enhanced when poor swimmers who ignored

---

[1] See J. I. Packer, 'Fundamentalism' and the Word of God (London: IVF, 1958), VII, 'Liberalism', pp. 146-68; 'Infallible Scripture and the Role of Hermeneutics', in Scripture and Truth. ed. D.A. Carson and John D. Woodbridge (Leicester : IVP, 1983), pp. 325-56.

his admonitions get into trouble. Am I then casting the Articles in a rescuer's role? Yes, I am. The deepest reason for producing them, over and above the short-term political gains of so doing, was to provide for the future the Anglican answer to the question, what is the gospel? Constitutionally, the Articles still do this. Since by biblical standards they answer the question correctly, and since the great body of Anglicans have drifted away from that answer, much to their loss, my enthusiasm will I hope be pardoned, however unfashionable it might seem. I really cannot think of any healthier course of study for Anglicans generally in these days than to analyze and assimilate the Christian message as the Articles define, display and delimit it.

Let none be put off by the fact that the Articles show their age, both in the language they use and in the secondary points they address. Of course they do. So do Chaucer and Shakespeare and Milton and Jane Austen and Emily Bronte. So do El Greco's paintings of Christ and the saints. So does the music of Byrd and Bach and Beethoven and Brahms and Bruckner. So do the tracks acoustically recorded by King Oliver's Jazz Band in 1923, which the late Hans Rookmaaker thought were the best thing since Bach. So does the miracle version of Elgar's violin concerto played by 16-year old Yehudi Menuhin under the composer's baton in 1932. So does the theology of Athanasius and Luther and Hooker and Owen and Edwards.

But dated form does not devalue classic substance, and classic substance enriches all ages, not just its own. Now the Articles have classic substance, and it is this that we need to assimilate today. Ask the Articles what the gospel message is, and they give you the following answer:

5.1.1.   The gospel is a message about God

God, Creator, Redeemer and Judge – the Triune Jehovah of the patristic creeds and all Christian theology prior to the sixteenth century. See Article 1 on God's eternity, perfections and triunity; Articles 2-4 and 15 on the incarnation, atoning death, bodily resurrection and impending return of God's Son; and Article 5 on the full personal deity of the Holy Spirit. Today the tri-personality and infinity of God are both called in question, as are Jesus' resurrection and return and the objective efficacy of his death. By starting with these fundamentals, however, the Articles show that if they are not stated right, then everything else is bound to be stated wrong, just because it depends on them.

5.1.2. The gospel is biblical teaching, about Christ and salvation

Sixteenth-century Roman Catholicism added extra books to the biblical canon and extra tenets to biblical doctrine; sixteenth-century forerunners of modern dispensationalism and situation ethics denied that the Old Testament speaks of the Christian salvation and that the moral law binds believers. Articles 6-8 respond to these ideas. Article 6 affirms the sufficiency of Scripture as a guide to salvation and identifies the 66 canonical books. Article 7 states the Christological, evangelical and ethical links which unify the two Testaments as one written witness to one organic revelation of eternal life. Article 8 lays it down that the reason why the three classic creeds should be accepted is not the church's say-so, but the fact that Scripture proves them true.

5.1.3. The gospel is a message about sin, grace, faith and repentance

Articles 9-18 spell this out elaborately, telling of our spiritual helplessness as sinners (Articles 9, 10). God's justifying of us by grace through faith for Jesus' sake (Articles 11-16), the plan of salvation in which justification is one step of a series (Article 17), and the exclusive claim that goes with the gospel's inclusive invitation (Article 18). The confessional character of these Articles appears in their use of the first person – 'we have no power' (Article 10); 'we are justified by faith only' (Article 11); 'good works ... cannot put away our sins' (Article 12); 'we doubt not but they [works done before the grace of Christ] have the nature of sin' (Article 13); 'all we ... offend...' (Article 15); 'we may ... fall into sin, and by the grace of God we may arise again' (Article 16); 'we must receive God's promises in such wise, as they be generally set forth to be in holy Scripture' (Article 17); 'holy Scripture doth set out unto us only the name of Jesus Christ, whereby men must be saved' (Article 18). It was intended that these statements should stand as the united witness of all Anglicans everywhere. The fact that they echo Augustine's technical vocabulary (original righteousness, original sin, nature, free will, good will, conscience, grace preventing and working with us) and use medieval technical terms as well (merit, supererogation, congruity) must not be allowed to obscure for us the fact that it is plain New Testament teaching that is being confessed. So here is the heart of the gospel as Anglicans do and should understand it: hell-deserving sinners are forgiven, accepted, and finally saved, by grace through faith in Jesus Christ the crucified and risen sin-bearer – faith which shows itself genuine by turning to God in true repentance and bringing forth good works as its new lifestyle.

5.1.4. The gospel is a message about the church

The gospel is a message about the church, the community of believers created by Christ that is called to live and worship under the authority of Scripture, with no unauthorized clergy or mystified members (Articles 19-24). The gospel heightens individuality but negates individualism, by stressing that the believer's new identity is corporate. Becoming a Christian is not a flight of the alone to the Alone, but a matter of being born into a large family; and being a Christian means sharing the life of that family according to the family code which Scripture sets out.

5.1.5. The gospel is a message about the sacraments

The gospel is a message about the sacraments, two family rituals whereby Christ confirms his promises to us and stirs up our faith in him and them on the principle that seeing is believing. The sacraments are not spells working magic, as has sometimes been superstitiously supposed; they are God-given signs sending signals to us about God's grace, and they must be received and responded to as such (Articles 25-31).

These five assertions sum up the thrust of the doctrinal Articles (32-39 deal with corollary questions of discipline and ethics), and even as brief a survey as this of the ground covered should convince us of our need to absorb their teaching. Is this the authentic New Testament gospel? Read the New Testament, and see for yourself. I do not know how any rational interpreter of the apostolic Scriptures can doubt that it is. For myself, I can echo with regard to these Articles the words of B. B. Warfield, who said on one occasion that he signed the Westminster standards gladly, and would teach their doctrine *consistently,*

> not, indeed, because commencing with that system the Scriptures can be made teach it, but because commencing with the Scriptures I cannot make them teach anything else.[2]

All sober and objective Bible students would, I think, have to say the same. So I urge that we who are clergy ought to have a conscience about expounding the Articles as a regular part of our ministry, and that layfolk should conscientiously labour to grasp the theology that the Articles contain – 'their system of doctrine', to use the common language of Presbyterians. This will of course mean study – study in which all clergy should be ready to help, and for which printed material is becoming available as well.[3] Let none grudge time and effort for this study. We shall all end up the stronger for it.

5.2. *Application*

By application I mean two things: bringing the Articles to bear both on current thought and on present-day living. Both modern doctrine and modern notions about worship and behaviour should be correlated with the Articles, as a step towards seeing how they square with the Bible. The church is called to honour God and do his will, which means that it must order its thinking and acting by

---

[2] B. B. Warfield, *The Inspiration and Authority of the Bible* (Philadelphia: Presbyterian and Reformed, 1948), p. 419.

[3] Latimer House itself sponsored the publication of a major exposition by Prof. Oliver O'Donovan, entitled *On the Thirty-nine Articles: A Conversation with Tudor Christianity* (Exeter: Paternoster, 1986).

the light of God's revealed truth, and one job that creeds and confessions are there to do is to keep revealed truth before Christian minds. Now the Articles are a church creed, as we have seen. They are not to be dismissed as a mere curio. They were drawn up to fulfil, under Scripture and alongside their other roles, the specific function of evaluating, correcting and where necessary redirecting whatever ideas the church at any time entertains. They stand as a constant challenge to deviationary views and a perpetual pointer to truer and more right-minded channels of thought. It is probable that the questions which most acutely agitate Anglican minds these days are those which plague the entire Western world – global peace, global development, global hunger, the nuclear threat and the nuclear deterrent, abortion, euthanasia, the mushrooming pornography industry, for starters – and it might be thought that the Articles can give us no help whatever in tackling them. But ethics is a branch of doctrine, and only when basic truths about God and his ways with us are clear can we hope to see the wise and right path for us to take in approaching these problems. Attention to revealed truth is never out of place, in fact. The Articles themselves are the fruit of such attention, and it remains an important and salutary part of our Anglican commitment to look at all competing views in the church (of which, as we know, there are many) by the light which the Articles shed on them.

Some, however, who would grant that the Articles guarded God's truth well enough in the sixteenth century, might still doubt whether they can give much relevant guidance today. The Articles, they would say, are more than four centuries old: how then can they bear on modern debates?

To this question there is, in my view, a two-fold answer.

First: so long as the Church of England centres its theological thinking upon the gospel; so long as it seeks a theology which is, to use the modern word, *kerygmatic* (ie. evangelical in content and evangelistic in purpose); so long as its chief desire is to understand and make known the good news of God's saving grace – so long will the Articles give us guidance at the point of our concern. For the clarifying of the gospel was their main aim, and their supreme achievement. To deny that the Articles speak to our time is tantamount to denying that the gospel itself does. To deny that the Articles can help the Church of England through its present-day problems is tantamount to declaring that the Church of England is no longer concerned about the gospel, and no longer wishes to focus attention on it. Anyone who took this line would be destroying the churchly identity of the Church of England, even if his public role was that of a professional theologian. It is a sad day for any church when its theologians lose touch with the gospel, for the job of theologians is to lead the church to see what it ought to believe and preach. Theologians strengthen the church when they study the gospel, but weaken it otherwise, by distracting it from that which matters most.

Should Anglican theology drift away from the gospel, no matter how learned and distinguished those who thus led it astray, the writing would be on the wall for the Church of England. No church can be healthy that majors in minors and forgets what really is fundamental. But an Anglican theology that is determined to cleave to the gospel will find the Articles as relevant as ever they were.

In their task of stating and safeguarding the gospel, the Articles were fighting battles that have had to be fought constantly down the centuries – the battle for the truth of the Trinity, for the deity of Christ and the sin-bearing significance of his death, for the sufficiency of Scripture and its supremacy over the church; the battle against Pelagianism, against self-salvation by works and effort, against authoritarian conceptions of the church, and magical views of the sacraments – and these are battles which will have to be fought again and again as long as the theological instincts of the fallen human heart remain as they were in the first century, and as they have demonstrably been ever since. In this regard also, as bulwarks defending basics which are always under threat, the relevance of the Articles is an abiding fact.

Second: the Articles do in fact deal in principle with many questions that had not yet arisen when they were drawn up. For a church's confession operates like the law of the land. It sets a standard and defines limits. It lays down rails for thinking to run on, and condemns by anticipation any future views that go off these rails. In its negative character it claims finality, saying in effect: 'never let your faith stray outside these limits; beyond the circumscribed area you will never find truth'. Thus, the Articles have permanent relevance as a test for post-Reformation theological developments, and as an index of the incorrectness of many opinions that have been canvassed in the Church of England during the past four hundred years.

An example of this is the doctrine of eucharistic sacrifice which the bishops at Lambeth in 1958 commended to the whole Anglican communion. Much work had gone into formulating it during the previous half-century. It rests on two basic principles: first, that the sacrifice of Christ is more than his once-for-all death on Calvary, and in some sense continues in the present; second, that the church's union with Christ is such that Christians are incorporated, not merely into his death and resurrection, but into his present sacrificing activity as well. The view it yields of what happens in the Communion service was stated by the bishops as follows:

> We offer our praise and thanksgiving for Christ's sacrifice for us and so present it again, and ourselves in him, before the Father ... We ourselves, incorporate in the mystical body of Christ, are the sacrifice we offer. Christ with us offers us in himself to God.[4]

In other words, we do not repeat Christ's sacrifice, nor add to it, but we do more than commemorate it; we participate in it.

The sense in which Christ's offering continues has been variously explained by adherents of this formula. Some have spoken of the suffering of Christ as a temporal revelation and reflection of something that ever continues in the presence of God. Some have spoken of the risen life that Christ now lives, and the

---

[4] *The Lambeth Conference 1958*, 2.84.

intercession that he now makes, as having the character of sacrificial self-offering. Some, with the Carolines and the Wesleys, have spoken of Christ always standing before God's throne, presenting, offering, or pleading his earthly sacrifice. Then the church's sacrifice is explained in terms of pleading Christ's death for the remission of our own and others' sins as we offer all that we are and have to God. This pleading is said to be a 're-presenting' (not a symbolizing, but a fresh offering or a 'making present again') of Christ's sacrifice to the Father in union with Christ himself as he re-presents it; and the church's corporate self-offering in Christ, within which our re-presenting of Calvary finds its place, is seen as the main purpose of, and the central action in, the eucharistic liturgy.

Of a piece with this is the fancy (it is hardly more) that the 'remembrance' (anamnesis) of Christ in the liturgy is directed Godward, as if Jesus' words 'do this in remembrance of me' had meant 'do this to remind my Father of me'.

Any who embrace any version of the Lambeth doctrine will naturally wish to reshape the 1662 Communion rite so that the church's self-giving may appear as the focal centre of the action, on which the commemorating of Calvary will then be predicated. To others, the 1662 order, in which the church's self-giving is response to the grace made known in the sacrament but no part of the sacramental action itself, will seem a better option. By their preferences here you may know their eucharistic theology. (ASB provides of course for both.)

The Lambeth doctrine was presented as an ecumenical breakthrough, transcending a historic tension between Evangelicals and Anglo-Catholics.[5] But how does it look when measured by the Articles? Directly, of course, the Articles say nothing about it, for it is a twentieth-century development. Indirectly, however, they say a good deal. Note the following

---

[5] This was a mistaken estimate, as was soon shown. See *Eucharistic Sacrifice* ed. J. I. Packer (London: Church Book Room Press, 1962.)

principles, laid down in Articles 25-26 (on the sacraments in general) and 28-31 (on the Lord's Supper in particular).

5.2.1. Both sacraments are signs of the gospel, with their meaning fixed by the gospel

The 'sacraments of the gospel' are 'effectual signs of grace' by which God works to 'quicken ... strengthen and confirm our faith in him' (Article 25). But to know what the gospel and grace and faith are we have to look back to Articles 9-18, which the sacramental Articles presuppose. Neither in the Articles nor anywhere else is sacramental theology a self-contained field of study. One's sacramental theology expresses one's doctrine of God and man, creation and redemption, sin and grace, the work of Christ and of the Holy Spirit, not to mention church and ministry; it is in truth the roof of one's theological house, supported by the rest of the edifice, and revealing by its shape the layout and structure of the building as a whole. So it is with the Articles.

5.2.2. Both sacraments are acts of God terminating on men

'signs ... by the which (God) doth work ... in us' (Article 25). As God is the chief agent, so his work is the chief action. The essential sacramental movement is from God to man, not vice versa. This is one major difference between a sacrament and a sacrifice.

5.2.3. Both sacraments proclaim Christ's work for and in men

Baptism is 'a sign of regeneration or new birth' (Article 27) through union with Christ in his death and resurrection; the Lord's Supper is 'a sacrament of our redemption by Christ's death', in which those united to Christ by faith partake of his body and blood (Article 28). Thus both sacraments exhibit Christ's atoning achievement and benefits which flow from it to us here and now.

5.2.4. Both sacraments are means by which God works faith

This point is basic to the truth (and truth it is) that they are *means of grace*. They convey the blessings they signify, so we are told, to those who receive them 'worthily' – 'rightly, worthily, and with faith' (Articles 25, 28). Right reception is believing reception. 'The mean(s) whereby the body of Christ is received and eaten is faith' (Article 28). As Luther said somewhere, faith makes worthy, unbelief makes unworthy. And the sacraments, in their character as visible words and acted promises, are God's instruments to 'not only quicken, but also strengthen and confirm our faith in him' (Article 25). They function as means of grace precisely because God makes them means to faith. The essential sacramental action is his coming to us sinners to call forth our faith through the sign and through that faith to impart to us the benefits of Jesus' death.

On this view, believing and receiving are the essence of sacramental worship. Those who have received sacraments should indeed give themselves to God, but such self-giving is a response to the grace made known in the sacrament and not strictly part of the sacramental action itself. That is the view clearly expressed in the 1662 Communion office.

Now the Lambeth doctrine of eucharistic sacrifice seems to contravene all four of these principles.

(i) This doctrine is not fixed by the gospel

This doctrine is not fixed by the gospel – not, at least, as the New Testament presents it. The Lambeth doctrine insists that Christ's sacrifice continues in heaven, whereas Scripture equates his sacrifice with his death and proclaims his work of offering as finished. Also, this doctrine labours to assimilate our self-offering to his, whereas Scripture does the opposite, stressing the uniqueness of Christ's vicarious sacrificial death and keeping it distinct from the sacrifice of praise and service which is our response to it. These emphases were not learned from the biblical gospel. If the concern had been simply to do justice to the New Testament, it is safe to say that they would never have been made.

(ii) This doctrine turns the Lord's Supper into an act of man terminating on God

The essential action ceases to be God's sacramental offering of Christ to men and becomes our sacrificial offering of ourselves with Christ to God. But this is to embrace an unbiblical fancy about the re-presenting of Calvary and to treat our response to the sacrament as if it were the sacrament itself.

(iii) *This doctrine makes the Lord's Supper a symbolizing not of Christ's sacrifice so much as of ours*

The service turns into a showing forth primarily of the church's devotion, and of the Lord's death only incidentally. But this impoverishes sacramental worship, not enriches it.

(iv) *This doctrine minimizes the function of the Lord's Supper as a means of grace*

On this view, the church comes to the eucharist to give rather than to get; not primarily to receive, but to offer itself in thanksgiving for what it has received already. This cuts across the view of the Articles, that the Lord's Supper is first and foremost a means for God to strengthen faith and communicate to believing hearts the fruits of Calvary.

It may truly be said, therefore, that four centuries ago the Articles passed a verdict on the Lambeth doctrine of eucharistic sacrifice. By anticipation they ruled it out as mis-shapen. To any currently attracted by it they suggest the question: is it not a poor thing compared with that which it seeks to supplant? Ultimately, of course, that question must be answered from Scripture, but surely it is the right question for us to face in this matter, and surely the Articles do us a service by pointing it up for us.

This is a sample illustration of the relevance of the Articles in assessing latter-day views. I urge that we should constantly apply them in this way.

5.3. *Augmentation*

But, when all is said and done, it is not to be expected that a sixteenth-century document will say all that needs to be said to guard the gospel and guide Anglican thinking today, and perhaps we ought to hope that by putting us under pressure God would bring us to the point of agreeing on a supplementary confessional statement for our time. I say 'by putting us under pressure' because it is only under pressure that significant creedal statements are ever produced. As Karl Barth wrote,

> Church confession is a Church event. The genuine Credo is born out of a need of the Church, out of a compulsion which in this need is imposed on the Church by the Word of God, out of the perception of faith which answers to this compulsion. What the confession formulates and proclaims claims to be Church dogma. In saying Credo it has characterized its pronouncements as those ... with which it challenges everyone to take up a position, to decision whether he can reject them as contrary to the Word of God or must accept them as in agreement with the Word of God. Here again it is Holy Scripture which is the basis of the certainty of the confession and the judge over it. [6]

That Anglican churches today, in their character as pillars and bulwarks of God's truth (see 1 Timothy 3:15), are under pressure from many sources and at many points is beyond dispute, but whether significant confessional responses will emerge from this situation remains to be seen. However, just as it would be an extremely good thing if such responses did emerge, so it is an extremely good exercise to consider what the content of such statements might be. That is Roger Beckwith's contribution to this Latimer Study, and for it I now hand over to him.

---

[6] Karl Barth, *Church Dogmatics* 1.2, pp. 624 f.

6. APPENDIX: SUPPLEMENTING THE ARTICLES

At the conclusion of Latimer Study 9, *Confessing the Faith in the Church of England Today*, the question was raised, whether the Articles, with the Creeds, were *adequate* as full and relevant expressions of the Christian faith in the context of the late twentieth century, or whether it might now be desirable to supplement them. This issue was briefly discussed as follows:

> We are often reminded today that the Creeds use the language and the thought-forms of the patristic age, in which they were drawn up. To a considerable extent, this language and these thought-forms are also those of the New Testament age and of our own age, but the expression *homoousios,* 'of one substance', is an exception. It does not occur in the New Testament, and in relation to present-day parlance it sounds materialistic. Yet those who modernised the translation of the Nicene Creed have found a rendering which sounds up-to-date, avoids materialistic overtones and is equally true to the original Greek. They have substituted the expression 'of one Being', and this is what appears in the Creed as it stands in the Rite A Communion service of the ASB. The expression can now be more clearly seen to be true to the teaching of the New Testament, although it is not in itself a New Testament expression.

> Few people today seriously entertain the idea of replacing the Creeds. If confessing the faith is a Christian duty, the Creeds are a biblical and ecumenically-acceptable way of carrying it out. Many Anglicans, however, would warm to the idea of replacing the Thirty-nine Articles, or even of discarding them without any replacement. It is fair to ask Why?

> The reply will probably come back that the Creeds are ecumenical, whereas the Articles are not. Yet the Articles are common to almost all the Anglican churches, and are one of the strongest links between those churches and continental Protestantism (now, like Anglicanism, a world-wide phenomenon). To play down our Reformation heritage is to ignore reality and to be untrue to history; it is also to display a

very selectively ecumenical spirit. Moreover, now that Rome itself is showing greater appreciation of the Reformation, it is doubtful whether any sort of ecumenism is helped by pretending to disdain it.

Another reply is likely to be that the Creeds are catholic, whereas the Articles are controversial. Certainly the Articles are controversial, but their tone is moderate, and their scope is limited. They do not pick unnecessary quarrels, or make unnecessary demands. Besides, two at least of the Creeds are themselves intensely controversial, as we have seen, though the errors against which they protest were once thought to be dead. Today, however, it is clear that the errors in question are not dead, if they ever were. Even the Regius Professor of Divinity at one of the older universities is reputed to teach his students that Arius was right and Athanasius was wrong.

Perhaps it will be said that the Articles are in rivalry with the Creeds. This, however, is clearly not the case. The Articles explicitly acknowledge the Creeds (Article 8) and repeat the substance of them (Articles 1-5). Moreover, the other great themes of the Articles, which are the authority of Scripture and justification by faith, are really just expansions on the credal affirmation that the Holy Spirit 'spoke through the Prophets' and on the credal topic of the 'forgiveness of sins'.

It will certainly be said that the Articles are dated. But why, then, are the Creeds not much more dated? It is true that the Articles deal with some questions which are not discussed today: even their great theme of justification by faith is not given nearly as much attention today as its prominence in the New Testament would seem to call for. However, statements on subjects which are not topical do not thereby cease to be true, and subjects which were topical yesterday may be topical again tomorrow.

The conclusion reached by the Doctrine Commission, therefore, in its *Subscription and Assent* report (1968), that the Articles should not be discarded, altered, or removed from the Prayer Book, and that the greatest change desirable was a revision of the form of subscription, was a sound one. It should be noted in this connection that resolution 43 of the 1968 Lambeth Conference is not in agreement with that report (as it states) but in sharp disagreement, and it is not therefore surprising that thirty seven of the bishops dissented from the resolution. If, however, the

Articles ought to keep their present status, and should only be treated more responsibly, is this all that the situation demands?

Obviously it is not. The Articles (like the Creeds) predate the scientific revolution of the eighteenth and nineteenth centuries, with its profound significance for the doctrines of creation and providence, and for Christian ethics. They predate the rise of the historical approach to the Bible, with its profound significance for the doctrine of biblical inspiration and the practice of biblical interpretation. They predate the demand of Anglo-Catholicism that the Middle Ages should be reassessed (and the demand of modern Roman Catholicism that the Reformation should be). We who live after these events inevitably read both the Creeds and the Articles with somewhat different eyes from those with which our forefathers read them, and when we repeat or subscribe them (though it may be with the firmest faith and the utmost sincerity), we do so accordingly. Of course, we are as yet far from having fully assimilated and assessed these events. There are still many doubts and much disagreement about them. Any approach to them is bound to be tentative, and it is probably still necessary for the different schools of thought in the church to assess them separately, before trying to assess them together. However, what in the long run we should be working towards is a fresh confession of faith, not as a substitute for the old ones, but as a complement to them and as a commentary upon them – interpreting them, applying them and adding to them, as our new situation demands. It is surely not too soon to make the attempt. There will doubtless have to be many attempts before success is achieved, but the voice of faith in the face of modern crises is what both the church and the world most need to hear.

The following is a modest first attempt in this direction.

6.1. A Supplementary Confession of Faith

6.1.1. The Transcendence of God

Though Article 1 does not mean to teach that God, who is Love, and whose Son is himself man, lacks sympathy with our human condition, it does mean to teach that God is independent of the world he has made. When the Bible speaks of God having his dwelling place outside this world, it may be speaking metaphorically, but it is using the metaphor best suited to our finite minds. Those who seek to substitute other metaphors, saying that God is 'the ground of our being' or 'develops with the world' are stressing his immanence at the expense of his glorious transcendence, and are verging on the philosophy of pantheism, which degrades God to the level of his fallen creation.

6.1.2. God and History

The Christian religion is intimately concerned with history. It speaks of God as active in the events of history, both through his ordinary providence, and through his miraculous intervention, exercised especially in the incarnation, virgin birth, life, death, bodily resurrection and ascension of his Son Jesus Christ. It also speaks of God as beginning history by creating the world, and as summing up history by judging the world, when Jesus Christ returns in visible glory. Though, in relation to events remote from human experience, particularly the creation and final consummation, the Bible may make more use of metaphorical language than usual, it cannot be said that even these events are altogether outside history, and in relation to events between these two terms such an assertion would be still less defensible. To call an event untrue or unhistorical, or to require that it be 'demythologised', simply because it is miraculous or otherwise incompatible with modern secular thought, is sheer unbelief. All that can rightly be required is that biblical history should be interpreted in accordance with the genuine canons of ancient historiography, at their highest ethical level.

6.1.3. Revelation

In all God's acts and works he is manifest to those who have eyes to see. Above all, he is manifest in the life of Jesus Christ, the incarnate Word. However, God's revelation would be partial and obscure without the interpretative words of Christ himself, the prophets and the apostles, which have been given permanent form in Holy Scripture. Moreover, because of fallen man's refusal to have the true God in his knowledge, God's revelation is wholly inapprehensible apart from the saving work of the Holy Spirit in man's heart. It is through the Spirit's work that man is personally confronted with God as Creator and Redeemer.

6.1.4. The Inspiration of Scripture

Scripture is not merely man's attempt to record God's revelation. Since it was written by the inspiration of the Holy Spirit, it is divine as well as human in character. The words of our Lord, the prophets and the apostles which are written in Scripture have the same authority as their spoken words. The history, doctrine and ethics of Scripture are the truth of God, who can neither err nor deceive. This truth was given to guide fallen humanity out of darkness into light. Tradition, the teaching Church and the human understanding all have a part to play in transmitting and applying the teaching of Scripture, but whenever they assert themselves against it they go utterly astray.

6.1.5. The Interpretation of Scripture

Since Scripture was written in human language, at particular junctures in history, it has a linguistic and historical background against which it must be understood. In this it is like any other literature. However, since Scripture was also written by divine inspiration, it has a unity and consistency which allows one part to be interpreted by another. In this it is unlike any other literature. It is the Holy Spirit who enables a man to understand Scripture, and the Holy Spirit has been at work in the hearts of a multitude of men in every generation. What others claim to have learned from Scripture must be tested by Scripture but must not be despised: it is by building on the labours of earlier interpreters that the Church makes progress in the understanding of Scripture. The Trinitarian and Christological definitions of the early Church and the Reformation teaching on authority and salvation have thus a permanent importance.

6.1.6. Grace and Faith

Grace is not a quasi-physical substance but is the personal favour and goodness of God to man. Faith is not mere intellectual belief but is trust, and trust in God involves belief of what he says. Since God speaks to us in Scripture about our salvation, to trust in him is both to believe that our sins are already atoned for through the cross of Christ, and to rely on him to accept us, preserve us, perfect us and glorify us for that reason.

6.1.7. The Grounds of Justification

The fact that believers are reckoned righteous by God on account of their faith does not mean that faith is a meritorious work. Faith comes from God and is pleasing to God, but the sole grounds of justification are the atonement of Christ on the cross, of which faith lays hold. Nor do the grounds of justification ever change. Though faith 'works by love', these good works are not the grounds of justification any more than faith itself is. Rather, they are proof that faith is living and true.

6.1.8. Universalism

The idea of universal salvation, against which Article 18 contends, still persists. But in fact the awful truth is abundantly clear from Scripture that not all men will be saved. It is also clear that non-Christian religions are to be regarded not so much as strivings towards the truth but rather as strivings against it: Judaism, and to some extent Islam, are special cases in that they are influenced by biblical revelation, but non-Christian religions in general are to be regarded as arising from a sinful perversion of natural revelation. No limits can be set to the dealings of the merciful God with individuals, even within non-Christian religions, but supernatural revelation sets forth Jesus Christ as the only Saviour from sin, and charges the Church to preach this gospel throughout the world as man's one hope in this world and the next. Dialogue with representatives of other faiths can assist in the removal of misunderstanding, but is no substitute for evangelism, and 'multi-faith services' are a form of syncretism, abhorrent to the one true God.

6.1.9. The Day of Salvation

The opportunity to repent and believe the gospel is limited to this present life, for men are to be judged by God according to the works done in the flesh, and to die in one's sins is to die without God and without hope. Those who die without the knowledge of the gospel will be judged by their response to such knowledge of God's will as they had by nature. To hold out the false hope of a second chance after death is to discourage repentance and to discourage evangelism while the opportunity for them exists. To pray that those who died unrepentant should repent and be saved after death is to ask what God cannot grant. Intercession for the dead is a practice which has no direct support from Scripture, and even when it is concerned with departed Christians, it often takes forms which imply either errors like purgatory or speculations like progress in grace between death and resurrection. As intercession for the dead is so liable to misunderstanding and abuse, the prudent course in public worship is for the Church to content itself with giving thanks for those who died in faith and praying for the living.

6.1.10. The Church Invisible and Visible

The one universal Church of God has two aspects, visible and invisible, but is not two churches. It is invisible in that God alone knows those whom he has chosen and whose repentance and faith are sincere. It is visible in that the public ministry of the word and sacraments, for which local congregations or churches gather, are visible. When a man repents and believes, which normally occurs through the witness of the Church, he is thereby joined to the Church invisible, and it becomes his right and duty to join the Church visible, or to confirm his existing membership of it.

6.1.11. The Unity of the Church

The smallest unit of the Church is the Christian family and the next in size is the local congregation, which binds together the Christian families and the Christian members of non-Christian families in a particular locality. However, all the congregations of

93

the universal Church have the same word and sacraments, believe in the same Lord and Saviour, and are inhabited by the same Holy Spirit, so fellowship and co-operation should not be limited to the local congregation. Still less should this be so where orthodox congregations of different polities exist in the same locality. Since episcopacy, presbyterianism, independency, infant baptism and believers' baptism are none of them unmistakeably commanded by Scripture, they ought to be no obstacle to the mutual recognition of ministries and sacraments, to close co-operation in Christian worship and witness, or to fellowship at the Lord's Table, even when it is not expedient to join in a single congregation. On the other hand, where there are fundamental differences of doctrine, close fellowship must wait until they have been resolved.

6.1.12. The Christian Ministry

In the New Testament, ministry is as manifold as are spiritual gifts, but there already exists within it an institutional ministry, to which outward appointment by the church is required, and not just an inward call from God. Presbyter-bishops, similar to the elders of the Jewish synagogue, were normal in the apostolic churches, sometimes assisted by deacons, and it is from these that the bishops, presbyters and deacons of later Christendom developed. The main tasks of the presbyter-bishops were teaching and pastoral oversight, not the administration of sacraments. The name 'priest' for presbyters was retained at the Reformation only because it is etymologically a short form of 'presbyter', not in a sacrificial sense.

6.1.13. The Ministry of Women

Women played an active part in the apostolic church, and it may be that female deacons are found in the New Testament, though female presbyters are not. The distinction is significant, because the diaconate did not until long after the first century become a first step to the presbyterate. And the presbyter has an office of authority (shown both by his title, which means 'senior man', and by the references to presbyters 'ruling'). St Paul teaches that the relation of headship and subordination between the male and female sexes goes back to the very creation, and should be observed both in the Christian family and in the Christian congregation. Though the church ought to set an example to the world, and not to follow the world's example, women set over men in civil society should be duly respected, since 'the powers that be are ordained of God'.

6.1.14. Christian Initiation

The New Testament attributes regeneration, the forgiveness of sins and the gift of the Spirit not simply to baptism but also to the word (or to faith, which is evoked by the word). Initiation, therefore, is not completed by infant baptism except in sacramental terms. On the other hand, the laying on of hands, which is not clearly commanded in the New Testament, is no necessary part of initiation: the only element in confirmation which is necessary is the candidate's personal response of faith to his instruction in God's word. Though, in the case of adults, reception of Holy Communion closely followed baptism in New Testament times, it is not an integral part of initiation.

6.1.15. The Eucharistic Sacrifice

The Holy Communion is nowhere described in Scripture as a sacrifice. The nearest the New Testament comes to this is by describing it as a feast upon Christ's sacrifice. Of the instituted acts of the service, only thanksgiving is elsewhere called a spiritual sacrifice, and this is a sacrifice which any member of the priestly people of God may offer, in private or in public. The idea that the eucharist is a ritual sacrifice offered by a ministerial priesthood is therefore quite foreign to the New Testament, as is ceremonial suggestive of such an idea; and when the further idea is added that this ritual sacrifice is identical with Christ's sacrifice on the cross, or with some heavenly sacrifice of equal or greater importance, the very foundations of Christianity are being overturned, and the language of Article 31, 'blasphemous fables and dangerous deceits', becomes appropriate.

6.1.16. Christian Morality

That love fulfils the Law does not mean that love can do without God's Law. Without the Law, love is blind. Love is the spirit in which God's Law is gladly obeyed. The restatements and reinterpretations of the Old Testament Law which we find in the gospels and epistles of the New Testament are therefore essentials of Christian morality. To relativize them in the manner of 'situation ethics' can only contribute further to the moral decadence which already exists. Whereas to take them at their face value, and to teach and live accordingly, will do more than anything else could to re-establish personal and social morality in the Church and in the nation.

6.1.17. Comprehensiveness and Discipline

The due order of the Church visible requires that it should receive those whom the Lord has received, not excluding any for trivial reasons, but also that it should check those of its members who openly practise wickedness or teach fundamental error. The Church of England has aimed to maintain this proper balance, not with entire success, as the separate existence of the Free Churches bears witness. The disciplinary Articles which conclude the 39 occasionally exalt probable opinions into certainties, and the uniformity which the 1662 Prayer Book requires in matters of indifference has proved too rigid for the consciences of some. Nevertheless, the fundamental departures from the biblical teaching of the doctrinal Articles and the Creeds and from Reformation principles of worship which have been witnessed since the beginning of the eighteenth century are a scandalous disorder, which theological ferment and decay of discipline explain but cannot justify. The restoration of a firm but loving discipline is something for which Christians should work and pray.

LATIMER STUDIES

CPSIA information can be obtained
at www.ICGtesting.com
Printed in the USA
BVHW071734070219
539735BV00002B/287/P

9 780946 307562